SWEETLY BROKEN

I bod ya!. Pleasure meeting you!
You are blessed and more than a
conquerer. Many will listen to you
because of godly wisdom you have!

08/06/10

SWEETLY BROKEN

Understanding the Pathway to Your Divine Assignment

Moses Asamoah Jr.

Foreword by Mark A. Stafford

To order additional copies of this book, contact:
Xlibris Corporation
1-888-795-4274
www.Xlibris.com
Orders@Xlibris.com
61203

CONTENTS

This book is dedicated to three outstanding men who have left an indelible imprint of God's anointing and grace in my life. They have gone above and beyond the call of duty, and it is a great honor for me when they call me, *son*! Without their sacrifice and investment, I will not be who and where I am today. This book is possible because of them.

Mr. Blackwell Moses Asamoah Sr.

I have known you all my life. You have always believed in me since I was a child, and I am eternally grateful and proud that you are my father! I admire your incredible wisdom, and thank you for loving me the way you do. Dada, I truly owe my life to you. I love you!

Pastor Daniel Yaw Klutsey Gedzah

You saw the passion in my heart and fanned it into flames. You saw into my future and pushed me to reach for God's best. I remember the day you asked me to close my eyes and imagine where I will be many years from then. I am living it now. Thanks for being there.

Pastor Mark A. Stafford

This must be a match made in heaven! When others overlooked and totally ignored me, you embraced me and loved me as one of your own. Today, I am standing on the shoulders of a giant, you. You are a precious gift to me and the Kingdom of God! Impossible is nothing!

FOREWORD

by Mark A. Stafford

We live in a world where the human default position is to seek peace, purpose and fulfillment through self-preservation, self-promotion and self-focus at all costs. There is no right understanding of Jesus' words ". . . whoever wants to save his life will lose it, but whoever loses his life for Me and for the Gospel will save it" (Mark 8:35). There is no true or core conviction that if we, like Jesus, make ourselves nothing (Philippians 2:7) and seek first the Kingdom of God (Matthew 6:33), that then and only then can we live the abundant life, the life to the full (John 10:10)

In *Sweetly Broken*, Pastor Moses Asamoah takes the reader on a paradigm shifting, eye-opening journey of self-discovery and introspection as he masterfully communicates the pathway to true greatness through brokenness before a Holy God. Pastor Asamoah not only makes the righteous argument, but he hits the reader squarely between the eyes with the truth, that to fully walk in the Jeremiah 29:11 prosperous plan of God we must allow and embrace the breaking-molding-making journey that God has ordained for our life.

Sweetly Broken is a "Must Read". As you savor each morsel of its life-changing truth, you will find yourself being truly transformed and divinely inspired with the turn of every treasured page.

I give my highest recommendation of Pastor Moses Asamoah. He is an amazingly refreshing man of God who walks in genuine integrity and a powerful, bondage-breaking anointing. I am convinced that if you read this book through the eyes of the Holy Spirit, you will never be the same and you will walk in a new level of true freedom and divine favor to the glory of God.

Rev. Mark A. Stafford
- Senior/Founding Pastor, Light Of Life Christian Center
- Founder/Executive Director, Light Of Life Ministries
- Apostolic Council/Vice-President, Bearers Of Light Ministries
- Chancellor, Pneuma Bible Institute
- Board Of Directors, Russians Reaching Russians
- Advisory Board, Accelerating International Mission Strategies

ACKNOWLEDGMENTS

Jesus is Lord! The opportunity to serve the Almighty God in Jesus' name is a life-time and eternal gift. My entire life is dependent on You, Jesus Christ, my Savior and Lord. It is because of Your love and constant breaking of my will and flesh that this book is born. Glory to God!

I must thank my dear wife, awesome ministry partner and greatest cheerleader, Delali. Your unwavering support and gentle encouragements made writing this book possible. You impressed on me not to worry and just keep it simple. So I will be simple: Eli, I love you!

I am also grateful to my life mentors: Wesley Burwell, Dr. Bramwell Osula and Dr. Joseph Umidi. Your candid questions and faithful accountability checks were safety nets. Our conversations strengthened my resolve to see this book to fruition. I salute you!

To all family and friends, thank God for your encouragements and thank you for your support and prayers. I am eternally grateful!

CHAPTER 1

BORN FOR SUCH A TIME AS THIS

The greatest confidence a man can ever have is from the conviction that he is born with a purpose and must fulfill a divine destiny. To discover and experience this destiny is an amazing pursuit that is lifelong and most gratifying. Beyond the accolades, the applause of men, and the selfish rewards that come with success, everyone desires to know and fulfill what they were placed on this earth to do. At the end of time, at the point of death you want to know that you made a difference. You want to know that your time here was not wasted.

> I don't know what your destiny will be, but one thing I do know: the only ones among you who will be really happy are those who have sought and found how to serve.
>
> —Albert Schweitzer

Your time on earth is defined by the events that happen between your birth and your death. Childhood experiences leave an impact and imprint on our lives. The grace to overcome the particularly negative experiences makes us even stronger to tackle other issues of life. Great people are great in part because they were presented with great challenges and opportunities. The circumstances surrounding your birth and death determine what you will be remembered for—the problems you solved and the ones you created.

I was born in Accra, Ghana, to Christian parents who invested greatly in my life. My father was especially instrumental in propelling me to where I am today. His gentle and firm demeanor and instruction was safety and direction wrapped into one. He is the most influential man in my life.

My birth was not an easy one. My mother was diagnosed with a fibroid of the womb, and the pregnancy was a difficult one. Put simply, I was at great risk. The level of risk increased to the point where doctors suggested that my parents choose between my mother and me. One of us was not going to make it. In as much as I know I am here for a divine assignment and had to be born at that time, the choice between my mother and I was difficult yet clear. If that was the only and final option, I would not make it.

The decision was obvious because I am the last of my mother's seven children. The sixth born, my brother, is more than eight years older than I; and my mother was forty-four years old when I was born. To leave a husband behind with seven children was not the humanly wise choice to make.

It is therefore the plan of God and a miracle by definition because my mom and I are alive today! It was at church that a prophetic word came that God was healing someone of a fibroid. I was safe because the Lord healed. I am here not because my parents needed another baby. I was not planned, and circumstances were not looking favorable either. It took the hand of God to direct my birth. He did so because I am on a mission to glorify Him, expand the kingdom, and destroy the works of the devil in Jesus's name!

Being the seventh of seven children and the fourth of four boys, I count it a great privilege to bear my father's first name: Moses. You would expect the first, second, or third son to be Moses Junior, not the fourth who by human understanding was an accident and came eight years after the supposedly "last baby" was born. I note that as God's divine impression of what He had for me to do. I love the meaning, reference, and association with the name *Moses*! Moses, the great leader and deliverer led Israel out of Egyptian slavery and to the borders of the Promised Land. Not only was this biblical connection powerful, but my father is also a great man I admire and am most privileged to bear his name.

In the same way, you too have a birth story that reveals God's plan for you, evident in the small details. Reflect on your birth story and hear the gentle whispers of the Holy Spirit for divine clues for why you had to be born at such a time as this. In addition to your birth story, consider engaging the season surrounding your birth. When you understand the season of your birth, you gain additional insight into your God-given assignment.

Joseph, the son of Jacob, was born in a season where *famine* in the entire land was inevitable. He was sold into Egypt as a young slave boy, and soon after the famine became unbearable. Joseph eventually became the vice president of Egypt with a specific mandate and wisdom to guide the country through and *out of famine*.

Moses, the leader of Israel, was born in *slavery* because his parents were slaves. He was not supposed to live because a "fibroid" enacted by the Pharaoh of Egypt required all Jewish baby boys be killed. Moses was stowed away in a basket and carried by water into the hands of the very ones he was going to fight to free his people. Bondage was the season surrounding Moses's birth, and the destruction of bondage was his assignment. He led Israel boldly and confidently *out of slavery*.

I was born in a season of national famine in Ghana. My memory of that time is as good as a baby can remember— none! Nonetheless, I know I am called by God to combat ignorance and resolve the famine of His Word to His people. What I felt in the physical is my spiritual impetus to feed the world with the Gospel of Jesus Christ. Death surrounded my birth; giving life to others through Jesus is my mandate!

Take time and reflect on the circumstances and seasons surrounding your birth. They hold divine clues to why you are born for such a time as this. Your name, your family history, your story are all strategically orchestrated to resound your God-given assignment. Take time to reflect.

BIRTHING A VISION

> *Before I formed you in the womb I knew you, before you were born I set you apart; I appointed you as a prophet to the nations.*
>
> *—Jeremiah 1:5*

God already knows His perfect will for your life. He knew you before you were born. His vision for your life is clear. You need only submit to His vision and how He wants to get you there. The vision is already there; you must discover it! God's plan for our lives, regardless of age, race, gender, geographic location, etc., follows similar foundational principles. The specifics are most certainly and thankfully different, but God's pattern remains the same. This pattern is revealed in God's vision for His son, Jesus Christ. It is safe to follow Jesus's pattern to understand our calling. Note these four truths that must hold true for all God-initiated and God-mandated visions.

The birth of Jesus Christ as recorded in the gospel according to Luke reveals these truths and principles. In Luke 1:1-35 the angel Gabriel appears to Mary with great news:

1. **"You shall conceive and bear a son . . ."** (verse 31)
Conception is critical to the beginning of every vision. At the moment of conception, a seed is formed with the potential and ability to replicate itself after its own kind. The seed principle is so powerful Jesus Himself ascertained that understanding the parable of the seed (Mark 4:13) was basic to understanding all His parables. At this point in your life, you are anxious to either discover or fully pursue God's vision for you. You are ready to conceive and give birth to greatness. But how does that happen?

2. **"The Holy Spirit shall come over you."** (verse 35)
Every godly vision must be conceived in the presence of God; otherwise it is not of God. Abiding in God's

presence over and over again is the only way to receive and conceive from Him. When you have paid the price of abiding and dwelling in His presence faithfully, God shares intimate details of His vision for your life. He must prove your faithfulness because He must prove your trustworthiness to handle the vision. Would you be a hireling or His child? This is critical because vision is important in the kingdom of God.

3. "His Kingdom shall have no end." (verse 33)

Time is a human concept. God is not bound by time. He was before time, is, and will be after time. He is the Alpha and Omega, the beginning and the end. So is everything and everyone born of God—perpetual and without end. God's vision for your life must agree with this principle. Any vision you have that has an end or possible end is not of God. Abide longer until you receive from your Creator a vision that cannot end because He does not end.

The disciples of Jesus Christ were brought before the Jewish Sanhedrin for preaching that Jesus rose from the dead and that He was the way to the Father. Before any further accusations could be hurled, Gameliel, one of the most respected in the group, asked the disciples to be dismissed for a moment. He wanted to address his comrades. Gameliel said:

> Men of Israel, take care what you propose to do with these men. For some time ago Theudas rose up, claiming to be somebody, and a group of about four hundred men joined up with him. But he was killed, and all who followed

him were dispersed and came to nothing. After this man, Judas of Galilee rose up in the days of the census and drew away [some] people after him; he too perished, and all those who followed him were scattered. So in the present case, I say to you, stay away from these men and let them alone, for if this plan or action is of men, it will be overthrown but if it is of God, you will not be able to overthrow them; or else you may even be found fighting against God. (Acts 5:35-39)

The proof of a godly vision is that it never ends. If it ends, it is not big enough and it is not of God. The prophet Isaiah confirms in Isaiah 9:7, "There will be no end to the increase of His government or of peace, on the throne of David and over his kingdom, to establish it and to uphold it with justice and righteousness From then on and forevermore . . ."

Expect the vision the Lord had placed in you to go on from generation to generation. God is concerned about this generation and the one yet to come. He wants people that He can continually bless through and have the seed of His vision bear fruit perennially!

4. "The Power of the Most High shall Overshadow you." (verse 35)

The unending nature of a godly vision is because it goes beyond our ability into God's ability. Overshadow has the illustration of fully covering and overcoming. Whatever you can accomplish with your ideas, wisdom, connection, and resources does not qualify as a godly vision. Godly visions are overpowering and overshadowing. They are fulfilled, "not by might, nor by power but by the Holy Spirit" (Zechariah 4:6). Your relationship with the Holy Spirit is the ignition and engine to propel you and bring God's vision for your life into fruition.

It's God's vision for you, not your vision.

Your God-given call and vision will transform individuals, families, communities, nations, and cultures. These are the convictions and commitments you should have regarding the vision:

1. It is POSSIBLE!

> Impossible is nothing! "*For nothing will be impossible with God*" (Luke 1:3).

"*The righteous will live by faith*" (Romans 1:17). I can do all things through Christ who strengthens me (Philippians 4:13). No eye has seen, no ear has heard, no mind has conceived what God has prepared me (1 Corinthians 2:9). I overcome because I have God with me. By God's hand, I will run through a troop and leap over walls (Psalm 18:29).

2. It requires FAVOR and I GOT IT!

I am a highly favored child of God. The Lord goes ahead of me and makes every crooked path straight. Like Joseph,

I am favored no matter where I find myself. The favor of God surrounds me at all times. Before I ask, I have because God is with me. Like Ezra, Nehemiah, and Daniel, I have favor even in foreign lands. I am highly favored!

3. MY LIFE REVOLVES around IT

I am a trustworthy and faithful steward. I guard my heart because out of my heart flows the issues of life. Because of God's vision for me, I choose wisely where I go, what I hear, what I see, and who I associate with. My entire life discipline is focused on faithfully executing this vision. I will not prostitute God's vision. I will not be lazy. Just as Mary's life changed and revolved around the seed she conceived, my life revolves around God's vision for my life.

4. I RECEIVE GOD'S VISION!

Be it so unto me according to Your word, dear Lord. I will trust and obey. You teach my hands to war. You, O Lord, lead me in the way that I should go. You order my steps. I will obey You! Your promises for me are yes and amen! You are truly perfecting that which concerns me.

FOR SUCH A TIME AS THIS

It is wise to acknowledge and understand that the methodologies and ideas that were revolutionary decades ago, even a year ago, will soon be inapplicable. Ignoring this is simply naïveté. A new generation is rising. A new culture has risen. And like the days after Joseph's death, a new Pharaoh has arisen who does not know Joseph, you, or our God. The vastness of communication media and worldwide connectivity will soon make the fax machine, e-mail, and desktop computer obsolete.

You are born for such a time as this! I am born for such a time as this! Our birth and life experiences have equipped us to effectively engage this time. Using all available media, we must communicate the Gospel of Jesus Christ without fail and without compromise.

Godly visions for our time do not bake faster than God's plans direct, despite the urgency of the moment. Neither do they avoid the godly principles discussed earlier in the chapter. For a vision to be born of God, without end and effective in expanding the Kingdom of God, the Holy Spirit is integral from conception to birth to growth to multiplication. There are no shortcuts to godly visions. Times are different, but the truth and principles remain the same. Jesus Christ is the same yesterday, today, and forever!

Are you ready to engage the Holy Spirit in a life-long adventure concerning God-given vision for you? He is waiting and longing to begin today.

MAKE THESE DECLARATIONS

- I am a fulfillment of prophecy.
- God has a plan for my life.
- My assignment is a solution to someone's problem.
- What God says and sees in me will surely come to pass.

- The Holy Spirit is my best *friend*.
- I am born for such a time as this.
- I will fulfill God's vision for my life.
- I will abide in the *presence* of God.

CHAPTER 2

SMALL BEGINNINGS

Your life is a unique one. Not in any way less unique than mine.

> No eye has seen, no ear has heard, no heart has
> conceived what God has in store for those who
> love Him.
> —1 Corinthians 12:9

You are divinely located at birth and through all your life experiences. Every experience in your life contributes to the fabric of your identity and purpose. To charge forward into the future without totally understanding and acknowledging your past experience is unwise. Unfortunately, it is common for us to have a desired future and race toward it without counting the cost and taking an inventory of what we currently have.

Suppose one of you wants to build a tower. Will
he not first sit down and estimate the cost to see
if he has enough money to complete it?

—Luke 14:28

These experiences can be collected from your own
memory or from conversation with those around you. You
will be amazed by how information you gather from others
about your experience will empower you to truly understand
who you are, where you're coming from, and where you
are going. So ask, ask, and ask. Gather all the information
you can, and the pieces of your life's tapestry will come
together.

You want something but don't get it. You kill
and covet, but you cannot have what you want.
You quarrel and fight. You do not have, because
you do not ask God.
—James 4: 2

As I share with you my experiences, listen for similarities
in our stories. Also note the differences. I share these with
you so you do not diminish the value of any experience no
matter how insignificant they may have seemed or seem
now. They all count. Reflect on where you were at the stage
of my life story and write them down. Here are my stories,
my reflections, and God's revelation through them.

THE ANNIVERSARY

My birth was miraculous as you know. The timing, season, and circumstances surrounding my birth were simply God-directed. Truly, by the grace of God, I am who I am today.

> But by the grace of God I am what I am, and his grace to me was not without effect. No, I worked harder than all of them-yet not I, but the grace of God that was with me."
>
> 1 Corinthians 15:10

At two years old, on my parents' wedding anniversary, I refused to eat that morning. My siblings tell me it was weird for a baby not to want to eat breakfast, and you'll agree. I also agree! It was a Sunday morning, and during the service, I neither complained nor cried for food. After church, I was still fine. I am told that it was later in the afternoon that I came to my mother and asked for something to eat. Little did I know, I was fasting for the first time in my life. This experience, when I later knew about it, fueled a passion in me to fast for weddings in my family. Of course I would not announce for whom I was fasting. That defeats the purpose. I know it was for a divine reason that I fasted though I may never know it. Thank God for the opportunity to express my love for my mother and father at such a tender age.

REFLECTION

- God redeems and uses your life experiences for His glory no matter how long ago they happened.
- What you loved to do as a child is key to your assignment. It came natural to you, and you enjoyed it.
- Fasting is great for your spirit, soul, and body. When was the last time you fasted?

THE PRODIGAL SON RETURNS

The first and only time my father spanked me was with a cane (switch) for getting "lost." I still laugh at my arrogance and overconfidence at age four. Right after school one day (kindergarten), my buddy and I had the sudden urge to visit our friends in other neighborhoods. I quickly changed my clothes, and off we went. We left my house around 3:00 p.m. Though my older brother admonished me not to go anywhere, I bluffed him. "I will be right back," I said. We visited our friends and totally enjoyed it but completely lost track or, more accurately, had no concept of time. When I finally returned home, it was almost 8:00 p.m. My parents and siblings had been looking for me everywhere. I walked through my neighborhood and to my home with great confidence. I cannot remember the reaction of anyone else, but I remember what my father did. He took the switch and laid four heavy stripes on my overconfident backside.

After much crying, I went to my father's bedroom to inquire what I had done so terribly to deserve such a punishment. I would never forget what he said because it is the foundation of one of my life's core values. My father simply responded, "What would have happened if I died? Who would take my place?" I am the last of seven children, fourth of four boys. Why would he be so concerned about me taking his place? I carry this in my heart every day. I understand what it means for a father to love his son. I did not read about it; I experienced it myself.

REFLECTION

- What my father said again two decades later confirmed and solidified my experience at age four. He said that if anyone messed with me, they mess with his heart. Having such a faithful and loving example of fatherhood was a clue to my assignment. I too would be a father to many, and I must show them that same love and commitment.
- My God-given assignment is to reflect the heart of my heavenly Father. "To love Jesus Christ and teach others how to love Him."
- In a class project, each student was given time to reflect and spend time with God. In my reflection, I told God I wanted to represent all of Him. His response was, "No, you can't. I am too much for you. I have called you to express my heart." With tears in my eyes, I remembered what my earthly father had said, and my childhood experience took on greater meaning and significance. Thank you, Jesus!

MR. PRESIDENT

In the ninth grade (junior secondary school, form 3), I had the honor of being nominated to run for the student body presidency. The school prefect is responsible for student activities, campus cleanliness, assemblies, etc. At thirteen years old, my leadership skills were limited to Sunday school and the kids in my neighborhood. Excitement over the opportunity was diminished by the reality of the responsibilities that the presidency entailed and required. The candidates were given a week to prepare our campaign speeches to the entire student body. I did what I thought was enough preparation. On the day of the speech, the nominees were called forward. I was second in line. When I got up to speak, I drew a blank. I had an obvious stutter, and all my stammering lips said was, "My name is Moses, vo . . . vo . . . vo . . . vote for me." The other nominees followed. The votes were cast and the ballots counted. I placed third and was entrusted with the school compound with the title and responsibilities of compound overseer.

Regardless of my first election loss, I embraced my new role and flourished in it. That was the beginning landmark of my leadership journey. You should know that my loss in the election was to a boy much taller than me named Jimmy Carter (no connection to the president). My other leadership roles were on a smaller scale as class prefect, in charge of all functions in my class, except teaching of course: book keeping, cleanliness, discipline, etc. I approached leadership the same way I approached my academics: hard work. I saw school work as a challenge and refused to be discouraged, intimidated, or defeated by any academic problem. "I can do it," was my attitude.

REFLECTION

- Losing that election showed me I need to prepare better. Academic success does not necessarily equal eloquence. Preparation and practice are key ingredients.
- Never despise small beginnings. Though I did not win the grand prize, this election experience launched me into public speaking. Seeing the crowd excited me. With more speaking opportunities, I gained confidence in what I had to say. A wise man once said, "A [every] long journey begins with a [single] step."
- I was not ready to be school prefect. It would have overwhelmed me. God knew my ability and what I could do. I rest in the truth that I cannot do all things, but that which I can do I will do with excellence.
- Give your best in whatever you do. Your experience in your current position is the preparation for your next promotion. Do not be sloppy, and don't take it for granted.

DRUMMER BOY

One of the most influential women in my life is Ms. Kafui Boadzo. Her smile and simplicity as she taught made every lesson appealing to me. Whenever I knew it was her turn to teach kids in church, my joy, though not outwardly expressed, was very, very high. Ms. Kafui gave me the foundation I have for my assignment. I still sing the songs she taught with such exuberance and remember the verses she made us repeat over and over again.

There were times that none of the Sunday school teachers were present. The children had already gathered in our classroom. When there was no teacher, I naturally took charge of the class even though I was not the oldest. I did what I remembered of Ms. Kafui's teaching. We sang songs like "We Are Traveling to a Land," "Peter, James, and John in the Sailing Boat," and "Ezekiel Prophesied to the Dry Bones." I had my beginning as teacher in Sunday school. It was there that my calling as a pastor began taking shape. It was there I preached my first sermon, and my pastor confirmed the teaching grace upon my life.

It was also at this church that I faithfully set up worship equipment before services and put them back after services. I have no doubt in my mind that it was through my service that God initiated the call. The call or assignment comes one and only one way: SERVICE! To ignore or seek ways around faithfully serving is to circumvent God's process. God does not honor that, and the result will be a fluffy ministry/call/assignment without substance, having a form of godliness but lacking the power of God.

As I served, I also observed the drummer on the worship team. I would stand behind him while he played. When he got up, I sat down quickly and tried to imitate what I had just seen him do. One day, the main drummer did not come to church, so I was asked to play. My feet were shaking, and my heart was beating fast. As nervous as I was, I played through. With more opportunities to play, I became better and better. This was the beginning of my music life: the little drummer boy. I was fourteen years old.

REFLECTION

- Service is the way to a fulfilled life and successful completion of your assignment. No other way!
- The foundation of a building of any assignment is crucial. The faithfulness of Ms. Kafui helped me develop a solid foundation for my life.
- If there is something you want to learn to do, observe those who are doing it right and succeeding. I watched, observed, and learned from Ms. Kafui and the drummer. By doing so, I learned to do what they did and was able to repeat it in their absence.
- Your calling is an opportunity presented to you. What opportunities do you have now? What are you doing to walk in it? The opportunity could be a clue to your assignment.

AREA PASTOR

Another of the many small beginnings I had was in Ambassadors of Integrity Good News Club (AIGNC). To fully appreciate AIGNC and its role in my life and ministry calling, I'll share its history with you. AIGNC was born out of Ambassadors of Integrity Christian Club (AICC). AICC was organized by young adults in the neighborhood. They met weekly for worship, prayer and Bible study. It was an accountability group mainly for young Christian professionals. As a high school student and hungry for more of God, I joined them. After a couple of times with the group, God laid it on my heart to begin a similar group for middle and high school students in the neighborhood. After much prayer, I hesitantly approached the leader of the adult group. He embraced the idea, and we decided to meet on Saturdays at 6:30 p.m. at the same location as the adults. I was thirteen years old, and that was the beginning of Ambassadors of Integrity Good News Club. My peers flocked to it, inviting their friends from all over the neighborhood. Soon, Saturday nights saw the gathering of over thirty, sometimes forty, youth singing, worshiping, and praying. Some of my finest memories come from that time.

While AIGNC was going strong, God birthed another vision within me. Every day on my way home from school, I walked through a neighborhood. Our house was on the hill, and this neighborhood was at the foot of the hill. Whenever I went through, I saw children about three to six years old just running and playing around. God said to start meeting with them. So every Wednesday night after dinner, I went to them and shared the songs and stories I learned from Sunday school. They enjoyed the action songs and memory verses. God moved in their lives. Eventually, some of the children of Valley Kids Church joined AIGNC on Saturday afternoons. Praise the Lord!

REFLECTION

- The willingness for my leader (AICC) to embrace my idea of AIGNC is the epitome of godly leadership.

Empowering young leaders and birthing visions that win souls is the responsibility of all mature church leaders.

- The most lasting relationships are those formed in the presence of God in prayer, Bible study, and fellowship. My friends from AIGNC are still connected today.
- God presented me with an opportunity to exercise and implement what I learned from Sunday school. When you pray, God gives you a seed, an opportunity to bear fruit. How are you using what you've learned? What opportunities are before you? They are clues to your assignment.

ACADEMIC SCHOLAR

One aspect of my life that I have always taken seriously was academics. Academic discipline and success were important to me because I knew it was a testimony to others. At least it was an opening to share the Gospel. For example, at middle school, students in Ghana had to take the Basic Education Certificate Exams in twelve subject areas. Their grades from these exams determined which high schools admitted them. I studied day and night for these exams. I loved school and was truly encouraged by my father to excel to the highest possible level. It is fair to say that I also wanted to make my father proud. I love him very much! When the results of the exam came, I had received the highest distinction possible in all twelve subjects. With such stellar grades, I could choose whichever high school I desired to attend. My dad had previously chosen St. Thomas Aquinas Secondary School for me. Aquinas Secondary School, as it is commonly known, is highly respected but at that time was not one of the elite schools. Trusting God and honestly, a little disappointed, I agreed to attend Aquinas Secondary School. In my time at Aquinas, I was careful about balancing school and ministry. I faithfully participated in ministry opportunities but was anything but ignorant of the importance of studying consistently and preparing for examinations. I also enjoyed helping my juniors in understanding mathematical concepts they might have been struggling with.

REFLECTION

- The one question I was asked most in my first year at Aquinas Secondary School was why I went there. It was not until several years later that I discovered the answer myself. Read my next new beginning, "The Apprentice," for the answer.
- The goal of academic excellence goes beyond beating everyone when it comes to grades, though that aspect was fun. Excellence is not a comparative word. It is subject to the individual. Your excellence differs from mine. Your excellence is the product of your best effort and hard work. Only you can answer the excellence question. Are you being excellent, giving your best in every area of your life? Don't compare yourself with others, don't point fingers; just answer the question!
- Education means to draw out. Education, regardless of what field it is, is meant to draw creativity,

wisdom, and inventions out of you. Be faithful with
the educational field you have in your hand.

- To truly know something, teach it to someone else.
Teach someone else, and you have served them the
gift of your experience in a seed.

THE APPRENTICE

It was an honor and privilege to serve and be taught
by Pastor Daniel Yaw Klutsey Gedzah. As a freshman
at Aquinas Secondary School, Dan took me and a few
other guys under his wings. He taught us what it meant
to be a true man of God. The spiritual disciplines were
daily practices for us—fasting, Bible reading, prayer, etc.
After school on several days each week, he would teach us
and answer our questions. He invested in us. The other
musketeers were Enoch Adjiri, Samuel Appiah, Alfred
Nyarko, and Moses Quaye.

What Pastor Dan pulled out of us is priceless. With
tears in my eyes, I beg, plead with, and admonish you to
find your spiritual mother or father and serve them. One
of the greatest enemies to your call is prematurely moving
ahead without your father's or mother's blessing. It has
handicapped many because they have nowhere to call
home. You cannot be in authority unless you serve under
authority. You cannot be a father to another in the faith
unless you have one.

You are sweetly broken when you acknowledge that you
are incapable of doing it all by yourself. Serve! Pastor Dan
honored me by naming his son after me. Ms. Kafui Boadzo

developed my foundation; Pastor Dan strengthened and gave me confidence that I too can make a difference. I consider him a partner in ministry today.

REFLECTION

- Find someone you respect and serve them. Let them impart into you that which you can never receive from books and by yourself.
- To receive the blessing of your mentor is to receive the benefit of their wisdom, anointing, and hard work without the pain and suffering they went through for it. The only costs to you for their anointing are the following: time, loyalty, faithfulness, and service.
- I came to Aquinas because any other top-rated high school would not have had Dan Gedzah. I came to Aquinas to find my first spiritual daddy. Locate your Dan today!

I have shared all these small beginnings with you because they play a vital role in my current make-up and the plans God has for me. Had it not been for these small beginnings, I would not be where I am today. As you reflect and record your "small beginnings," notice the hand of God in your life the whole time. God said He will never leave you nor forsake you, and He hasn't. I have had my share of failures and disappointments. You have too. Comparing who got it worse is futile and a step backward. Let's press forward for the price of the high calling of God in Christ Jesus. The good and bad experiences together create you and what you are passionate about. Reflect on and write them down. Just as after many years, I recognized why I went to Aquinas, you too will understand as you reflect.

DECLARATIONS

- I am a true servant of God.
- I do not despise small beginnings because God is perfecting that which concerns me.
- I honor my spiritual leaders.
- I am willing to serve them because they follow the Word of God.
- My assignment is revealed in my life story; God have and will always be with me.
- I count my failures as necessary on my journey to a fulfilled life.
- I do not judge myself by my surroundings because I am born of God.

CHAPTER 3

THE ANATOMY OF A CALL

One of the most lingering questions of future leaders and those interested in understanding the call of ministry is "How do you know you are called?" The mystery associated with the call lies with the need or desire for certainty before responding yes to such a demanding and life-changing commitment. The question also exposes a general misunderstanding that all callings are ministerial, or that a call is always a major deviation from one's natural life circumstances.

Several leaders I know are effective in sharing the Gospel of Jesus without being called into full-time vocational ministry. Their daily lives and professions are their calling, and through those avenues they fulfill their God-given assignments. Others like me had a drastic change of course in order to fulfill my call. I switched from chemistry and a path intended to end in a medical doctorate to full-time pastoral ministry in a church. In this chapter, we explore the anatomy and basic ingredients of the call, whether it's full-time ministry or full-time vocational ministry.

QUICK SUMMARY

- A call is a commitment to a way of life.
- NOT all calls are to an office in the church.
- Your call could be in your current vocation.
- Some calls require drastic changes, but that's not always the case.

In observing biblical figures who were called, we notice two types of callings. The calls are undoubtedly from God, but the channels and responses are not the same.

In the first kind, the response to God's call is that of rebellion, denial, or excuses. Jonah ran opposite to the direction God sent him. Gideon did not want to accept it and created a different scenario to disperse his call. Moses said he was a stutterer and could not speak.

The second kind of call involves an overwhelming experience that cannot be denied. It is so profound that the one being called knows beyond all doubt. For example, many had an angelic visitation. Ezekiel was shown deep revelations he never could have known. Your response to God's call falls in some degree in these two categories. It might even be a combination of both.

The response to the call of God is not regulated by God. Your response to God's call in your life is your choice. I have realized though that with a submitted heart, the journey is a lot easier. Why not say yes now and avoid all the "hard seasons" and then say yes eventually? Just a thought!

There are five themes I have identified in the call from God. Please take note of any more themes you identify and send me an e-mail.

COMMON THEMES IN A CALL

1. GOD-Initiated

Our independence as individuals unfortunately causes us to assume a sense of invincibility. We plan our days and pursue our desires expecting that it shall be so because we want it. The call of God usually interferes with our plans and pattern of thinking. Even a call that is not especially different from one's own desires is God-initiated and involves a clear time when you acknowledge the call. God is the one who establishes His kingdom, and He calls on us when the time is right.

2. GOD States the "WHAT"

In order to solicit a clear response, God sets the stage with why the call has come and why at this particular time. From His understanding, God lays a clear foundation and His analysis of the situation.

3. GOD Gives a General "HOW"

It is almost cliché, but the truth remains that if God gave us the total picture of how the call was to be administered, we, in our independence and free-willingness will charge ahead of God. That's why the general how is all that God gives. Even in the general, the assignment usually feels impossible. But with God all things are possible. The details of how God's vision will be achieved come with consistent obedience. Details are privileges.

4. For a Specific Season; To a Specific People

The call is God's answer to a person/people's cry for deliverance. Your call is not another "find something for him/her to do." It is strategic in the planning's of God and to a specific person or people. God's greatest asset is His children, and every assignment is designed to either liberate them or empower them into greater levels. Honestly, no one called can save the world. When Jesus died and rose again, He made a way for all to gain access to the Father. The executive announcement and distribution of this good news (Gospel) is the sum of the call God has for each of His children.

5. **Solution to a Specific Problem**

It is unlike us to aspire to be all things to all people. If we could solve the world's problems by ourselves, we would. The truth, however, is that we cannot. Your call is not to fix every single problem the world has. Your vision and assignment would also not fix every problem. It will have great impact in solving a particular and specific problem. The exciting and equally difficult task in discovering and implementing the vision is to stay focused.

Let's observe these themes in the lives of Gideon, Paul, and Mary (mother of Jesus)

GIDEON (Judges 6:7)

Gideon was a Benjamite. He lived in the time when Israel was under the oppressive rule of Midianites. Food was scarce, and the fear in the land was evidenced by Gideon crushing grapes in secret.

THEMES	BIBLICAL REFERENCE/ EVIDENCE
GOD-INITIATED	Judges 6:11, an angel sent from God came to him.
GOD STATES THE WHAT	Salvation of Israel
GOD GIVES THE GENERAL HOW	God will be with Him (verse 16)
TO A SPECIFIC PEOPLE	Israel (verse 13)
SOLVE A SPECIFIC PROBLEM	Midianite oppression

PAUL

Paul was a Pharisee and a Roman citizen by birth. He was named Saul until he had a powerful encounter with God. Paul learned total submission to the authority of Jesus Christ and became a true apostle of the Gospel.

THEMES	BIBLICAL REFERENCE/ EVIDENCE
GOD-INITIATED	Light from heaven shines and knocks him off his horse.
GOD STATES THE WHAT	Paul, you are persecuting Me (My people). Arise go to the city.
GOD GIVES THE GENERAL HOW	Bear my name (verse 15).
TO A SPECIFIC PEOPLE	Gentiles
SOLVE A SPECIFIC PROBLEM	Persecution of Church, and Israel's denial of Jesus as Messiah

JONAH

Jonah was called by God to bring a redemptive message to Nineveh. It was a message that provided salvation if the people repented. Jonah tried to avoid the responsibility, but God had made His choice. He learned it was much easier to surrender to God than to flee.

THEMES	BIBLICAL REFERENCE/ EVIDENCE
GOD-INITIATED	Word of God came to Jonah (verse 1)
GOD STATES THE WHAT	Go to Nineveh
GOD GIVES THE GENERAL HOW	Cry against it
TO A SPECIFIC PEOPLE	People of Nineveh
SOLVE A SPECIFIC PROBLEM	Wickedness of city

MARY (Luke 1:22)

Mary was a virgin chosen by God to conceive and bring forth Jesus Christ. It was an honor for her to be the mother of the Messiah. It also brought her great pain as she saw her son go through a horrendous death on the cross. To Mary, this was a life commitment.

THEMES	BIBLICAL REFERENCE/ EVIDENCE
GOD-INITIATED	An angel came to Mary
GOD STATES THE WHAT	Birth of the Messiah
GOD GIVES THE GENERAL HOW	Conception by the Holy Spirit
TO A SPECIFIC PEOPLE	Jesus Christ Himself
SOLVE A SPECIFIC PROBLEM	Sin of all mankind

Everyone's assignment is unique and different from all others. Our personality and geographic location alone distinguish us from others. God has a plan for you and calls you for a specific time, people, and problem. As you reflect on the what, who, how of your call, it is important to understand these truths about your call:

- It is greater than you and seems overwhelming.
- It requires complete dependence on God.
- It stems out of your personal weakness or failings.
- With God, you can do it.

CALLED OUT OF AFRICA

You are where you are geographically because it is part of God's plan for your assignment. Take a purposeful look on your place of birth and place(s) where you lived during your childhood. Those locations added specific attributes to you and together created the individual God needs for your specific assignment.

Moses, the deliverer of Israel, was born in Egypt; he learned the culture of the land and its leadership. Moses became very influential and respected in Egypt. Then he changed locations from the palaces of Egypt to the shepherd's tent at the backside of the desert in Midian. In this place and location, Moses learned humility and received pastoral training, a sharp contrast to the dictatorship he knew in Egypt.

Then in time, the call came, and Moses was given marching orders to no other place than Egypt. It was here that the call will be manifest. Moses's knowledge of Egypt was important. Likewise was his experience herding sheep and watching the night skies alone with desert sand or rocks for a bed. God used Moses's natural and geographic locations to shape and adequately equip him for his assignment.

Like Moses, I too was born in Africa. My cultural heritage remains Ghanaian no matter where I move to. The lessons I learned from family, school, and communities in Ghana all contribute to God's call for my life. I moved to the United States as a teenager to a wholly different culture and way of thinking. I studied in American universities and lived in various communities. My experiences in America taught me cultural sensitivity. My training as a pastor all happened in the United States. God uses both Ghana and America to shape me for my call to Africa. I am called out of Africa for Africa.

Never despise a geographical move. The blessings of God accompany such moves. Submit to God and embrace the new location. It surely holds a major component of your assignment. Don't miss it because you whined and complained. When I finally acknowledged the call of God in my life and began searching for answers, the major question I had was "how do I know I am called?" And when will that time be to step out in it? You are probably there right now. In my search I consulted with my then senior pastor who shared the six C's of the call with me. Thought you would like to know.

THE SIX C's OF THE CALL

1. THE CALL—It is the inner convictions and record of when you heard/felt God separate you from what

was normal to you or when He asked you to separate yourself from all others (persons and things) to be closer to Him.

2. CHARACTER—Would you pass the integrity and honesty test? God is working on your character as we read this book right now. Can you identify the before and after pictures of your character?

3. CAPACITY—fortitude, ability to endure the pressures and discomforts of the call without wavering or being distracted.

4. CONSTITUTION—consistency and ability to stay with

5. CONFIRMATION—affirmation of those around you

6. COMMISION—hands laid on you by pastors and elders

THE CALL

The call comes in a clear, audible voice; a strong impression on your heart; and through clear and obvious signs. When the Lord calls, your very peace is engaged until it is resolved. Everything about your life changes to accommodate this call. Remember that the assignment may be what you're doing. Nonetheless, the call comes to initiate God's takeover and to empower you to operate at a divine, God-enabled level.

I always knew I was going to serve in the church. My plans, however, were to succeed in the medical field then do ministry. In my first year in college, God said, "I have called you to be a doctor of people's hearts, not of people's bodies." I heard it, put it on the shelf, and kept on with my routine schedule. I stayed involved in church and campus ministry. My personal time with God was mostly very consistent. It was the summer before my senior year that I knew clearly in my heart that God wanted me to abandon my pursuits in medicine. I could not ignore it any longer; I could not deny it. I prayed and cried and prayed and even tried to negotiate with God. I prayed something to the effect of, "God, I will make $80,000 in the first year of my profession. I will give to the church and support ministry." God simply asked, "Do you think you can build my church with $8,000 per year [my projected tithe]?" I responded, "No!" Since that fateful evening, I knew the time to answer the call was amazingly critically near.

In my senior year, everything in my life changed to accommodate this new passion I had for God, His Word, and His people. I stayed up late studying the Bible and woke up early to do the same. The excitement to be with God was unprecedented. I prayed, read, worshipped daily, and enjoyed it all. I didn't feel at any moment that I was missing out on anything. I was consumed with passion for Christ! The call is not just a desire to serve. It is an all-consuming divine request that requires a clear, definite response. As one of my college mentors told me, in response to angst and internal battle, the call "is the expulsion of a higher affection." What used to matter no longer does. The only thing that mattered was saying yes to the Master. I will share more of my internal wrestling with you in the next chapter.

CHARACTER

Character is defined as a distinctive quality and has its root meaning in "to scratch" or "to engrave." Your character is your unspoken, non-verbal identity, the engraving that is noticed by everyone without you mentioning it.

We have heard it said numerous times that your true colors will eventually show. You may have heard, "You can fool all the people some of the time and you can fool some of the people all the time, but you cannot fool all the people all the time." Who you truly are will truly come out. The specifics of character include but are not limited to your temperament, gentleness, manners, responsibility, reaction to people, etc. The strength of character lies not simply in the display of these characteristics but more importantly in the authenticity and truthfulness behind what is seen.

Authenticity begins as a private work of the heart. It begins with answering the questions: "What do I do when no one is looking?" and "Who am I when no one is observing?" Before you judge the outward display that everyone sees, check your inward foundation that no one sees. Is what we see what we get (whether we are in your presence or not)? One of the greatest battles of one who is called must fight is the battle within. Am I truly who people see that I am? Am I truly who I say that I am?

Character is an identity issue. Character's respectability comes from the fact that it is always consistent in all situations. Two situations that I truly believe reveal true character are *praise* and *promotion* and *trials* and *testing*. An individual may be patient and kind when life is normal. Observe how they respond to praise and promotion. Do they remain the same as true character would, or would they change to being full of pride? Also observe how a sweet, helpful, and encouraging person fades in the face of trial and testing. True character is the genuine fruit of processed thoughts and positive life changes. The wrestling and brokenness is what makes character true. It is not affected by the environment or changes in it. THOSE WHO ARE CALLED MUST SUBMIT THEMSELVES WILLINGLY to the processing of God until His identity is engraved in their hearts. Those who skip this heart-wrenching process only prove themselves to be false, unreliable, and inconsistent. Allow the brokenness God initiates to break away your will and your flesh. When the process is well under way, then you qualify to represent Christ in whatever field He calls you.

CAPACITY

Capacity is the ability to hold. How much can you hold and for how long? The call to serve the Most High God and His people is not a trivial assignment. People are not like computers from which you can expect certain output depending on your input. Humans are complex and cannot and must not be treated as machines. What distinguishes man from all other creatures is the higher ability to think and the greater freedom to choose. No man is under another's rule or control. "There is a time when a man rules over another to his own hurt" (Ecclesiastes 7:8). Basically, no one owes you anything, and you own no man. God holds all humanity. You have a mission to a specific person or group of people. How much of their complex lives can you endure knowing that no one owes you anything and you do not deserve rewards for your call?

A great percentage of capacity is self-control. Yes, the call involves bearing others' burdens, and one who has no self-control cannot be trusted with the lives of others. How much of you do you have under control? If you cannot contain and discipline yourself, your people capacity is low. A high capacity is not given at birth. It proceeds from an intentional and conscious effort to expand the potential within. Simply put, transform POTENTIAL into true CAPACITY!

A couple of weeks into my second grade year, I was promoted to the third grade. I was excited but very apprehensive about engaging this new chapter in my life. Obviously, my teachers noticed my potential to succeed at a higher academic level. However, potential did not mean guaranteed success. I had to discipline myself with hard work to make my potential into true capacity—the ability to hold my ground and standard at this new level. My first social studies exam was quite a scene. I cried when I saw the exam, overwhelmed with the fear that I could not pass it. My third-grade teacher called my second-grade teacher to calm me down. In reassuring me, he addressed my potential. He could not address my capacity because that was my responsibility, not his. I had never been in third grade, so he had no prior record or reference point. My success at the third grade was dependent on me taking my potential and adding hard work and discipline. And that's what I did. I studied five nights each week and became top of the class. My potential was now confirmed in evidenced capacity.

Your call requires you to go through a similar process of breaking, discipline, and reformation. God's plan for you is no light thing. You must, therefore, prove your capacity at the highest point before the call. You never know when the time to answer the call would be. The newest next level could be the call. Your final place before you hear the call could be your current academic pursuit, place of employment, family situation, etc. Prove yourself able and trustworthy.

Potential is fluff; capacity is tangible and real. The saddest word used in the English dictionary is *potential*. It is the highest form of what could be. May it never be said of you that he had potential, but rather, may it be said of you that you proved and fulfilled your potential. God expects us to solidify our capacity. He told Jeremiah,

> If you have raced with men on foot and they have worn you out, how can you compete with horses? If you stumble in safe country, how will you manage in the thickets by the Jordan? (Jeremiah 12:5)

The call is greater than where you are now. Build capacity where you are, for you will need it to fully execute the assignment.

CONSTITUTION

Constitution simply describes what you are made of. It is different from character and capacity. Your constitution is what dictates your character and determines your capacity.

It is what you become when you process potential in capacity. The fruit or evidence of what you are made of (constitution) is your character. Character is a product of your constitution.

Let's explore this further. Say I watched a football game in which the Indianapolis Colts won, and I had to tell you about it. "Great game" gives you a general concept of what the game was but provides no details. You would at least want to know the score and maybe number of touchdowns, yards, etc.

Here's another example: You invite someone to your house and do not give them your address. Simply telling them your house is a two-story in Virginia Beach would be of no help to them.

And here's a final example: I take you on a tour to Ghana and decide to point out the president to you. Saying "He's the tall black gentleman over there" doesn't help you at all. There are a lot of tall black gentlemen in Ghana, believe me. You might even question if I knew what I was talking about. Details are important.

In that same trend of thought, do you know the details that make you unique? What are your strengths and weaknesses? What's your leadership style? What motivates you? How do you respond to conflict? You must know what you are made of. Your discovery of these constituents is a matter of time, intention, and process. Knowledge of your constitution is critical to your call and effective execution of your assignment. Improving and enhancing your constitution increases your capacity.

A motivational-gift assessment I took revealed I had a strong administration gift. I had always considered myself weak in that area or, more truthfully, I didn't want anything to do with it. With the discovery that I had the administrative gift, I was no longer excused from it. I know what I am made of, and I totally embrace it. A major component of my current ministry role is administration. I cannot imagine ignorance of this gift.

Here are some ways to discover what you are made of:

- Ask those closest to you what they see in you. Compile a list of the most common observations from their responses.
- Take a motivational-gift assessment test.
- Perform a personal inventory of your life and what you are made of.
- Take time to reflect.

CONFIRMATION

He who walks with the wise shall be wise but a companion of fools suffers harm.
     —Proverbs 13:20

Plans fail for lack of counsel, but with many advisors they succeed.
     —Proverbs 15:22

At this point in time, you are probably anxious about answering yes to the call. You have a general idea of what the call is, and you are considering the when. A vital step now is to receive the wisdom of those around you. I say this emphatically but with some reservation. It is of the utmost importance to seek counsel, but be discerning and careful whose counsel you seek. Not all who smile at you understand you or necessarily like you or want the best for you.

Rehoboam, the son of Solomon, was confronted with a situation during his reign as king of Israel. Read 1 Kings 12. For counsel he consulted with the advisors who served his father—older men, with wisdom tempered by great and many years of experience and sometimes suffering. He also consulted his peers, who had a great deal of youthful exuberance and lacked the understanding of reality and wisdom needed. Unfortunately, he rejected the wise counsel of the old men and heeded the counsel of his friends. The tragic result was the splitting of his kingdom. He gained two of the twelve tribes of Israel while ten of the tribes left with Jeroboam. Needless to say, wise counsel or the lack thereof has great consequences. Ask for counsel, but be selective from whom you receive it.

It is important to seek the counsel of respected men and women of God. By respected, I mean those who are recognized to be people of character and known for their biblically based leadership. The input of your spiritual mother or father is also very important. We discussed their value in chapter 2. Last but not the least, among those you should consult, talk to your current pastor. If you have been willing to sit under his teaching and follow his leadership, you should honor him by asking his opinion. He knows something about you that will help you gain further clarity, confirmation, and confidence in whatever direction you finally decide to take.

COMMISSION

This last *C* is a formal step that some would take; others may never need to take this. Commissioning combines the first five *C*s and places divine approval and seal on it. This is a very critical step required for those called into full-time vocational ministry. It has three important components.

1. Prayer by apostles and elders. This is what we usually call ordination. The apostle Paul admonished church elders to lay hands suddenly on no man (1 Timothy 5:22). To have hands laid on you for ministry is a clear mark of being set apart.
2. Impartation. By the laying on of hands, there is the spiritual impartation of gifting, anointing, and authority. Beyond what is seen is the supernatural impartation that one gains after commissioning.
3. Public recognition of ministry. What God has called you to do is now clear to all. It provokes a new level of respect accompanied by a greater level of responsibility and accountability. People now treat you differently and expect you to be trustworthy and faithful.

After commissioning, your life is never the same. You have new authority, grace, responsibility, and the demand of a new ministry journey. So help you God!

CHAPTER 4

NOTICING THE CALL

As we walk along through these processes of reflecting on and better understanding the call, be rest assured that God has a plan for you even if you do not fully comprehend it now. The call of God on your life will bless both those near and afar. Trust God to lead you and guide you. He never fails.

Do you remember the moments and times when you felt the weight of a higher purpose? Remember the times when you knew in your heart that God has a purpose for you? What about those confirmations from acquaintances and strangers alike that brought a smile (okay, a smirk) to you face? It is time to recollect them and see God's handiwork at hinting to you the plans, purposes, and confidence he has in you.

One source of the commendations I often received was my superiors at work. In various ways and at the weirdest times, they came and encouraged me.

"You'll make a good pastor. I see that in you."—Bill,
Xerox

"That Moses, he's a special kind of guy."—Russell,
Staples

"You're a scholar and gentleman."—Store Customer

"You are something else, how old are you?"—
Employer

All these affirmation may seem to be simply kind
gestures, but they are truly God engineered to lift your
head up and brighten your day. On the other hand,
there are those bosses who make it their personal mission
to discourage, torment, and abuse your dreams and
personality. Though infuriating, they also have a place in
God's plan; ask Joseph, the son of Jacob. He got the abuse
from his brothers at home and ended up in a pit. Then
he got it from Potiphar's wife—false accusations, though
Joseph was the most trusted in the house. He got it in jail
when those who he served got better and forgot him. He
did all this while serving a foreign hand, away from his
father who loved him so dearly. The words of affirmation
and the coat of many colors were nowhere to be found. Yet
he persevered. And he conquered!

Another source from which we gain confidence of
God's plans for our lives is prophetic words. I believe
in prophecy wholeheartedly. God is a prophetic God,
for "He calls things that are not as though they were"
(Romans 4:17). Prophetic words come to CONFIRM
what God has spoken to you. They reveal the truth that a
great God knows and cares about the littlest details of our

lives. Prophecy is encouraging, edifying, and awesome! Nonetheless, prophetic words are not instructions from God. They are CONFIRMING words. We must embrace prophetic words and respect them, but do not use them as mandates.

When you receive a prophetic word about God's plan and call for your life, listen attentively. Write it down and pray about it. If it doesn't make sense, pray and visit it occasionally until God reveals more clearly to you. In the fullness of time, all will be made clear. If it makes absolute sense and confirms your heart's desires, still be cautions. Pray and hear clearly from God; this time not for relevance but for timing. Timing is as crucial as the instruction itself.

Ask Moses, the prince of Egypt. Moses enjoyed the best education in the then-known world. He wore the best clothes and lacked nothing. One day Moses feels the yearning to further investigate his heritage. To some assuring degree, he knows he's an Israelite. Moses analyzes the situation and exclaims, "Aha! I know why God has made me a person of authority in Egypt. He wants me to save the Israelites from bondage." With a renewed boldness, Moses begins to see Egypt in a different light. He watches the Israelites more. He is more merciful and favorable in pardoning offenses. Soon Moses grows weary of the palaces and feels them closing in on him. He now wants to interact with slaves more instead of drinking and making merry with the Egyptians. One day Moses takes a stroll to the fields. There he sees an Egyptian beating one of his people, with disgust and anger for "those" Egyptians; and being tired of "their" ways, Moses launches at the Egyptian and kills him. Feeling justified and untouchable, Moses begins more patrols, develops more schemes, and feels without a shadow of a doubt that he is fulfilling God's call for his life. When Pharaoh found out that Moses killed an Egyptian, he wanted to kill Moses. Without warning and planning, Prince Moses escapes through the desert to Midian to serve as Pastor Moses. His congregation was the True Sheep of Midian Assembly.

Timing must not be disregarded. God works in χιρος (time in moment), and we work in κρονος (time in orderly sequence). Prophetic words must be subject to God's plan of fulfillment. Take them as part of noticing the call, not a mandate to execute the call.

GENERAL GUIDELINES FOR PROPHETIC WORDS

- Prophecy is biblical. Believe in the exercise of the gift. See 1 Corinthians 12:1-11, 14:1.
- Prophecies are conditional and require obedience.
- Prophecies are trustworthy, not based on its fulfillment but rather on the character of delivering vessel.
- Prophecies are not mandates; they are viable confirmations.
- Prophecies require time and timing. Hear God!
- When prophecies don't make sense, pray and visit them often until God reveals their meaning or purpose.

LIFE EXPERIENCE

These stories I am to share with you about my life may be common or similar to yours. During the times the stories took place, I had no understanding of the call of God on my life. I was simply living my life to please God the best I could. Notice the hints of God's call through the stories. Reflect on your stories as well and see the formation processes of God's call on your life.

CAPTIVE AUDIENCE

During my tenth- and eleventh-grade years at St. Thomas Aquinas Secondary School, I mainly used public transportation. I rode two buses to school, two buses from school, and walked several miles in between. On numerous occasions, by the impression of the Lord, I would sit farthest to the front of the bus. As soon as the bus pulled out of the depot and the conductor had received the bus fares, I would rise from my seat and begin sharing the Gospel. People slept, most listened, and a few gave their lives to Jesus Christ. Even on days that I determined not to speak, the Holy Spirit compelled me. I continued this in the neighborhoods. I would not shut up about Jesus Christ.

HINTS OF THE CALL

- No fear of people, no care for their approval.
- Obedience to God first and at all cost.
- Sharing the Gospel as foundational to every ministry call.

PROFESSOR

I have always had the hunger for simplicity and understanding. I always simplified my class notes to levels that made sense to me. I took it further. It is my firm belief that you truly understand a material when you are able to teach another. Then again, that is the special gift of teaching, which not everyone has.

Children, including my peers, will come around to my house where I had prepared a classroom setting: the board, chalk, eraser, chairs, tables, etc. I explained in simple terms concepts that their teachers could not help them understand. I enjoyed that very much. This experience was common to me from the first grade and through my academic career.

HINTS OF THE CALL

- I am a teacher in gifting, preaching and leadership.
- Simplicity is important because the Gospel is not complicated.
- Experience something before you expect others to do the same.

THE LONE RANGER

My tenure in high school was a very powerful experience. There is no doubt that God was preparing me during that time for who I am today and whatever I will be in the future.

The typical high school years are ninth, tenth, eleventh, and twelfth grade. I completed my sophomore and junior years in St. Thomas Aquinas Secondary School. Upon arrival in the USA in December 1996, I had missed half of the year (my potential senior year). I repeated the last half of the eleventh grade and began my full senior year in September of 1997. I had to get used to everything—the clothes, the language, the nuances, etc. My academics were never an issue however.

Due to some circumstances beyond my control, I only had one lunch meal between February 1997 and June 1998. My adaptation to the situation was to fast and pray. I spent most of my lunch periods on the track field studying God's Word and praying. My confidence grew in God, knowing that regardless of my new environment I was still His son. My earthly father's wise saying, "It is not where you are but who you are," became my motto. I lived it in spite of my peers laughing at my clothes, insulting my accent, and basically looking down on me. I knew in whom I had believed. I knew who I was in Christ, and nothing would change that.

Out of my time in the presence of God grew the passion for the Gospel. So I began to explore the process of establishing a Christian club in the school. After finding a sponsor and location, my friend Omari Boateng and I began Restoration Christian Club in T. C. Williams High School. It was a great victory! Today, some of my friends who I used to "bother" with the Gospel are mighty men and women of God! No seed of God's Word is ever wasted.

HINTS OF THE CALL

- Separation from others and what seems to be fun is part of the call. Being alone with God and enjoying it is a basic requirement.
- God uses your circumstances and needs to shape His call.
- Fruitfulness is born out of intimacy; your ministry success is directly linked with your time spent with God.
- Restoration Christian Club was another "church plant" and confirmation of the church-planting call on my life.

STUTTERER TO STATESMAN

I love to talk. I talk a lot. I have always talked a lot. As a young boy, I had a terrible stutter. It hardly prevented me from communicating, but nonetheless, it was clearly evident. In T.C. Williams, I decided to join the debate club and become a member of National Forensic League (NFL). I trained for Lincoln-Douglas debates (moral and social issues) and for student congress. At my first competition, I lost my first five debates. In student congress, I was still learning the "whereas . . ." of bills. With much training and practice, I improved. In my senior year, I won the MVP award for the debate team. The last three months of my high school career were very exciting. We went from competition to competition trying to earn enough points to qualify for the next level, and we did. By so doing, I earned a berth to nationals. I was voted in by one female judge. The national championship was in St. Louis, Mississipi, in June. It was such an honor and a landmark moment in my life; I skipped my graduation in order to participate in this national competition. It was worth it! I ranked eighth overall in the nation at the end of the competition. That is my God! He took a stutter with a foreign accent and made his speech eloquent.

It was important that I mention my debate class as another crucial ground of preparation. I was the best extemporaneous speaker in a class of thirty to thirty-five students. My teacher, Mrs. West, noticed my gifting and wrote this note at the end of the semester: "To whom much is given much is required." I have much to give, so much is required of me. I cannot stop. I must not stop!

HINTS OF THE CALL

- Your greatest area of struggle is the great component of your call.
- All it takes is one person to believe in you.
- God transforms you into the vessel He needs. Surrender your life, trust Him, and let Him.

GOD'S DELAY

After graduating high school, I had great plans. I was on my way to be a neurosurgeon. The Ohio State University sent my admission letter a month before graduation. All plans, thoughts, and roads were leading to Columbus,

Ohio, the city of the Buckeyes. It was all excitement until I hit a financial wall. My financial aid was not well processed, and I could not afford the out-of-state tuition, room and board, etc. It was too much for my family, especially since my siblings and I had moved to the United States only eighteen months ago. Fortunately, I had to take a year off school against my will. I say fortunately because I now know it was God's handiwork in my heart and my life.

I got a job working as a cashier in a grocery store. I added another job working for a well-known office supply company. I worked these two jobs faithfully. I had never taken more than a day off school, so I wrestled with my future and why I was in such a situation. Then again, time spent in the presence of God uplifted me. I know God brought me this far in life and He would take me all the way. The heartburn about my friends going ahead of me eased. I was in a God-initiated delay. I embraced it.

It was during these months of two jobs, graveyard shifts, and dreaming about work in my sleep that I paid my first tithe. Wow! I bought my first computer and first sound system. I bought clothes and was able to give money away. It was incredibly fun. God used the delay to mature me, teach me customer service, and make me depend completely on Him. I became self-aware and self-confident.

During this one year hiatus from school, I remained faithful in church. I was at every worship team practice (drummer), every Sunday service (though I worked some Sundays), and every Friday-night prayer meeting. No matter our situation, our commitment to the things of God must not waver. In uncomfortable situations, we must press harder into the things of God. God's delays are truly fruitful when we embrace them.

HINTS OF THE CALL

- The call is not a race. Neither is your life success.
- Seasons of God's preparation will interrupt your plans.
- Your life is not your own.

From these few stories I have shared with you, observe the subtle truths about God's call in your life. You are inconvenienced, and the path is not as you planned it. Take time and notice the call of God throughout your life. God has always been at work, so you must learn from those moments to put your life today in true perspective.

CHAPTER 5

PROCESSING THE CALL

There is always the awareness that God has a plan for your life. As time progresses, you begin to sense that the plan is getting more specific. The actual details may not be clear, but your sensitivity to the call increases. Hiding or denial at this point is futile since you cannot even convince yourself to ignore the call.

So was my situation in the summer of 2002 when I was doing a research project at Mary Washington College. Back in my dorm room, I wrestled with God. I fought desperately to hold onto the comfortable dream, to my design of my future. Every reason to pursue my own way and simply bring God along was not working. In the midst of the wrestling, I knew the right thing to do. I knew the conclusion, but I still fought it. It seemed so unfair. And yet again, I knew responding yes to God was the best for me. God's NO to my plans was a YES to my destiny. I chose God's plan.

Very interestingly, around the same time, a relationship that I thought would end in marriage ended abruptly for many wrong reasons. In more ways than one, I was hurting on two fronts—losing my planned life and losing my planned relationship. I mention this because when the moment comes, God lays clear imprints on your life situations that you cannot ignore. It became clear that the journey had begun. He begins to separate from you people and things that are not necessarily bad but do not fit into God's plan for your life. When you observe the lives of biblical patriarchs, their moment of calling always involved a drastic change. For example, observe Abraham (instructed to leave Ur and separate from his family), Joseph (sold by his brothers into slavery), Moses (forty years in the wilderness), Elisha (sacrificing his oxen and leaving his family), and Jesus (leaving His heavenly glory to die for a people that opposed Him). Trust God during this season. Abide in His presence because He is the only One who brings any degree of joy, love, acceptance, and peace. Now, you are His.

Attempting to run away, deny, or ignore this time in your life is very tempting and part of the processing. You may be doing what I did. After all the undeniable encounters with God, I still pursued medical school. I got applications from universities and actually visited one of them. I updated my resume with all my college accolades. I personally do not fault anyone who may be going through this stage right now because the call is no joke and is a drastic life change. It is important to process the call. Hear God, pray, read, ask for counsel, hear God, ask for more counsel, hear God, and pray. You go through all these because you want your answer to be sure. That is part of the process. I must inform you, however, that your destiny will only be fulfilled when you say yes to God. So, here's a hint: the correct answer is "Yes, Lord!" Let's discuss some critical processing issues.

WHO? ME?

The plan of God is massive, and the call to serve Him exclusively can be overwhelming. You feel small and inadequate. Out of nowhere comes the sudden urge to improve yourself, as if to improve ourselves would convince God He made the right choice by choosing us. Your faults become more glaring, and you wonder why God will choose someone like you. Then comes the angst about the future: Do I have what it takes? Am I a true leader? Am I qualified? Would I be received? The answer is found in the Word of God

> The LORD did not set His love on you nor choose you because you were more in number than any of the peoples, for you were the fewest of all peoples, but because the LORD loved you and kept the oath which He swore to your forefathers, the LORD brought you out by a mighty hand and redeemed you from the house of slavery, from the hand of Pharaoh king of Egypt. (Deuteronomy 7:7-8)

> You did not choose Me but I chose you, and appointed you that you would go and bear fruit, and *that* your fruit would remain, so that whatever you ask of the Father in My name He may give to you. (John 15:16)

> The LORD will accomplish what concerns me; Your loving-kindness, O LORD, is everlasting;

Do not forsake the works of Your hands. (Psalm 138:8)

I did the same questioning of myself. Truth be told, we are not alone. Jeremiah said, "Alas, Lord GOD! Behold, I do not know how to speak, because I am a youth." God responded to Jeremiah:

> Do not say, "I am a youth," because everywhere I send you, you shall go, and all that I command you, you shall speak. Do not be afraid of them, for I am with you to deliver you. See, I have appointed you this day over the nations and over the kingdoms, to pluck up and to break down, to destroy and to overthrow, to build and to plant. (Jeremiah 1:7-10)

God said to Ezekiel:

> And you, son of man, neither fear them nor fear their words, though thistles and thorns are with you and you sit on scorpions; neither fear their words nor be dismayed at their presence, for they are a rebellious house. (Ezekiel 2:6)

DO I HAVE ENOUGH RESOURCES?

Another issue that suddenly takes on a high degree of importance is the funding of God's call on your life. How would we pay for this? How would I take care of myself? How do I care for my family? All these questions arise from the insecurity that we are no longer in control. Our plan has been altered and our confidence tampered with. God is the great Provider—Jehovah Jireh, and He would provide for your every single need.

The children of Israel left Canaan during a famine to go into Egypt. They came in with nothing but left with the riches of Egypt. Israel himself, back when he was called Jacob, fled to his uncle Laban. He got there with nothing but left with a caravan of wealth and riches.

Jesus paid taxes with money from a fish's mouth. When Jesus sent His disciples out, they went with nothing, and upon their return, He asked them if they lacked anything. They responded, "Lord, we lack nothing!" You too will lack nothing because God is your source.

> I have been young and now I am old, yet I have not seen the righteous forsaken or his descendants begging bread. (Psalm 37:25)

God pays for what he orders. Your call is an order from Him, and He will honor it. If you can trust Jesus with your eternity, you can trust Him with your lunch.

As I wrestled with the consequences I would face after responding yes to the call, the passion for God increased. It is vital to understand that the passion and excitement must be not for the assignment but rather for Jesus Christ. The desire to know God and become deeply acquainted with Him supersedes the call, which is only a by-product of your relationship with Him. Remember again, productivity flows out of intimacy. I will wake early and stay up late to spend time praying and reading my Bible. Jesus became my passion and obsession. The hunger to digest God's Word and abide in His presence was so strong it was intoxicating. Nothing else really mattered. Everything paled in comparison to the fulfillment I received from knowing God, being known by Him, and "taking hold of that for which Christ took hold of me" (Philippians 3:12).

With each passing day, I accepted my call and began looking forward to it. By faith, fully expressing my confidence and leaning totally on Jesus Christ, I knew that what I now have is more than I could have ever had if I had pursued pharmacy or medicine. Others close to me felt otherwise. They are entitled to their opinion. Many raised the money factors. Others raised concerns that I was too young. I was even called lazy! You will hear a lot of people who mean well but do not clearly understand God's call on your life. Others are simply frustrated because their plan through your life will no longer be. They can no longer control your life's outcome, and that irritates them. It is wise to acknowledge what is said; pray about it and hear God. The final verdict through it all is PEACE. When it's time, even in the midst of your questions and wondering, your heart will be at rest because you are in agreement with God.

PEACE

It is unfortunate that the typical definitions of peace are the following: absence of conflict, calm, quietness, etc. Those only partially illustrate what peace is. Peace is far beyond a still, quiet moment. Peace is resting in the midst of disorder because you know who is with you. The very presence of chaos is what defines peace. Without the riotous background, peace is indefinable. For example, Jesus slept soundly in the boat while His disciples panicked and frantically worked to save their lives. The situation was stormy, yet Jesus rested. In fact, he was fast asleep! That is peace! Your peace is not dictated by the absence of trial but rather in the midst of it because you trust God. Isaiah 26:3 says, "You will keep in perfect peace him whose mind is steadfast, because he trusts in You."

The Israelites were at the Red Sea with Egyptians bearing down strong on them. While some wanted to stone Moses, God told him to tell Israel, "The Lord will fight for you; you need only to be still" (Exodus 14:14). Death was looming, and the instruction was to be at peace. Peace comes before the trouble is over. You can be at peace when all is fine. True peace is resting in spite of the confusion. Even when your family, friends, circumstances, and the future are loud and seem daunting, you can be at peace and hear the call of your Lord.

The call is merely the beginning. Don't place the burden on yourself to make it manifest or to fulfill it. God is in charge. Take time to process, and then make a heart commitment to stand strong against all opposition that prevents you, or all propulsion that pushes you ahead of God. The day I totally gave up everything and stopped wrestling with God, and myself, ushered in a new season in my life. You have signed on the dotted line. Now what's next?

CHAPTER 6

YES, LORD! NOW WHAT?

It was spring of 2003, and I had reached the point of no return. I had made up my mind and heart to answer the call of God. At this point, I realized I did not have a plan for what to do next. I had written down my life plan for the next ten to fifteen years and basically knew how each year and month was going to look. Well, after answering the call I no longer did.

My first inclination was that I needed to study so I could be effective. I had preached and ministered and held leadership roles, but those experiences were not enough for where God was taking me. Ministerial and leadership training are important. Training may take on different forms, but it is a basic foundational requirement. It does not have to be in a seminary or Bible college. It could be under the tutelage and mentorship of your leader. Whatever form of training it is, an intense season of preparation is crucial to your success in ministry. Jesus spent thirty years in preparation for three years of ministry, and He knew the assignment the whole time. Your recent discovery requires and confirms that you MUST most definitely be trained.

I decided to attend Regent University in Virginia Beach, Virginia. The School of Divinity offered a master's in divinity that was perfect for me. I would concentrate my degree study on missiology—global missions. The excitement began to build again. I was making arrangements to move to Virginia Beach. It was something new and refreshing even though I could not predict the outcome. I was going with faith as my only possession. God was gracious to provide an apartment for me. I got note of this apartment about two weeks before classes started. All attempts to secure a place in previous months had failed. Getting this apartment was more confirmation that God was in this geographical and spiritual move. On January 4, I was sitting in my first class, Principles of Bible Study.

The classes were very good, and I enjoyed this new knowledge. It was definitely different from chemistry where the scientific method was the rule. The Holy Spirit directed my learning and provoked growth in me. The vision of what God had planned was coming into view, and I got it, or so I thought!

Taking the written ideas of things I wanted to do for God after medical school, plus a few new "revelations," I came up with my new vision for my life. I had fallen into the temptation of planning for God and asking Him to co-sign. I presented this new vision for ministry and my life to my academic advisor. My advisor was not simply a seminary instructor. He is a well-traveled, experienced, been-there-done-that missionary. I thought for sure he was going to love the plan and help me implement it as soon as possible. When he saw the documents (PowerPoint slides), he reviewed them without a smile. He then proceeded to tell me how puny, outdated, and non-visionary my plans were. He got up and left, saying I needed to think bigger and be more Kingdom-minded. Left sitting at the table, my eyes watered. I picked up my dream, got in my car, and drove around town, crying the whole time. After a few hours of driving and at one point crossing the border of North Carolina, I returned home and cried some more. I had given up my life dream of medicine to fulfill this vision and now there it was, shredded to pieces. Once again, I was left without a plan.

All that turmoil I felt was God-initiated. He called me; I did not call myself. It'll be His plan, not mine. After years of studying under some awesome professors, I understood how incredibly frail my plan was. I began to comprehend the power of synergy and partnership. Every strategy I developed thereafter included in part joining and supporting those already working in a particular field of ministry so as not to compete or reinvent the wheel. I learned that the Great Commission was to disciple nations, not just my local community. The plan of God is global and reaches the ends of the earth.

God would shred your plans because He has bigger and better things for you. Allow Him to process you and your plans because only then will you be part of His call and His team.

> But he knows the way that I take; when he has tested me, I will come forth as gold. (Job 23:10)

For you, O God, tested us; you refined us like
silver. You brought us into prison and laid
burdens on our backs. You let men ride over
our heads; we went through fire and water, but
you brought us to a place of abundance. (Psalm
66:10-12)

My academics progressed well. I trained as a professional
life coach because I wanted to effectively listen, draw out,
and empower others in their life journey. A few years later,
I became a professional life coach trainer. The opportunity
also arose to have a joint degree from the School of Global
Leadership and Entrepreneurship in Regent University. I
felt led by the Holy Spirit to do another master's degree
in organizational leadership. I signed up for my first
leadership class, and at the end of the semester, I was issued
a fat grade: F. Failing to do my work on time made that
grade unavoidable. Dreading to see that on my transcript, I
opted to switch to a master of education program instead.
The program looked promising until I heard God, as clear
as day, say, "No! Go back and fix your mess." I knew I
had to retake the leadership class and complete the entire
program as God had initially instructed. After a lot of hard
work, I successfully graduated with two master's degrees:
master of divinity and master of arts in organizational
leadership. I now know why God wanted me to go
back and fix my mess. Organizational leadership was in
preparation for what I do now and is in line with what I'll
be doing, God-willing. Remember, your Heavenly Father
knows best.

My studies were very relevant and truly fulfilling because I served in a local church and applied most of what I learned in class before I graduated. God allowed me the opportunity to serve at Light of Life Christian Center in whatever capacity was needed. I went from serving as a youth worker to senior associate pastor. During this journey, I have had a role in every ministry (except women's ministry) and filled vacancies until the right person joined the team.

I emphasize training and service because I know without a shadow of a doubt that they are the only pathways to fulfill your God-given assignment. You must be trained, and you must serve. It is through service that you learn to show the heart of Christ and are sweetly broken to be more like Him. Skip training and service and you become a liability and casualty of ministry. Insist on being mentored and prepared until the Lord who called you releases you. The maturity of your call is not of your choosing, and it has nothing to do with length of time either. It is God's call, and He chooses when, where, and how you are deployed.

One of the best examples of "Yes, Lord, now what?" was the relationship between two prophets of Israel, Elijah and Elisha. Below is a summary of that dynamic and divine calling. See in 1 Kings 19:19-21 and 2 Kings 2:1-15.

- God instructs Elijah to anoint Elisha as a prophet in his stead.
- Elisha places his cloak over Elisha while he is working the field and walks away. Elisha immediately understands and bids farewell to his family and friends.

- Elisha kills the oxen and uses their yoke for firewood.
- Elisha follows Elijah as his SERVANT.
- At the end of Elijah's life, Elisha begins his calling with twice as much wisdom, ability, and anointing of Elijah

Many feel ready to take on the world or see the need so great we want to begin now. The desire to see change should never overwhelm and lead us to abandon training and service. I have met, talked with, and know several men and women who were burned out because they were not prepared for the race of ministry. Training and service prepare your heart to do much more than you could under your own auspices.

Gehazi was Elisha's servant, but he was not faithful to neither his master nor to the call of God on his life. Tempted by the riches that Naaman, the Syrian general, offered, he falsely represented Elisha. His punishment was leprosy. What is worse, in my estimation, is the value of what he lost. If the pattern was to hold true, he would have received a double portion of Elisha's anointing, which was already double of Elijah's anointing. Do not become a spiritual casualty by misrepresenting your leaders for self-promotion or gain. Do not miss out on the power and anointing God has for you because you could not wait!

There is great wisdom in having a spiritual father or mother. I have both! In a multitude of counselors there is safety. I shall end this chapter with a summary of a message I preached titled, "Humility: Key to Activating Christ in You." Enjoy!

HUMILITY: KEY TO ACTIVATING CHRIST IN YOU

To walk in the fullness of God's anointing, you must humble yourself before your leaders. The Kingdom of God is a kingdom. It is not a democracy; we don't vote in the Kingdom of God. It's "Yes, Lord." To have the fullness of Christ in you, we must be like Christ when He said, "Not My will but Your will be done." He was able to share how He felt, but He said, "If that is your instruction, Father, so be it." How many times has your leader or pastor instructed you to do something and you debated with them, questioning whether they are truly hearing from God? God leads you to the place He knows will prepare and launch His plan for your life. Stay and serve!

> And he gave some as apostles, and some as prophets, and some as evangelists, and some as pastors and teachers, for the equipping of the saints, for the works of service to the building up of the body of Christ. And so we all attain to the unity of faith and to the knowledge of the son of God to a mature man to the measure of the stature which belongs to the fullness of Christ. (Ephesians 4:11-13)

The role of the leaders is to equip the body to do the work of ministry. Their role is to equip and empower and release all the fullness of God in you so that you can be the man or woman of God that He has called you to be.

God has chosen to anoint your leader (man or woman) to empower, to train, to equip the body of Christ. This is God's preferred choice and channel of ministry. That is how he has decided to bless and to impart his anointing. Unfortunately, there are two extreme attitudes toward leadership. The first is disrespect on one side: "I can read the Bible for myself. Who does he think he is? He's got a radio show and a TV whatever. Who is he? I can even preach better than he can." Behavior as such is the epitome of complete disrespect and dishonoring of authority. On the other side is when submission to a leader equates to man worship. When your leader's opinions transcend God's Word and Spirit in your life and decisions, you are in trouble. If someone sees you in that manner, stop them from worshipping you! Do not play God.

God has not called you to worship the man of God, and he definitely does not want you disrespecting them either. When we align ourselves with God's kingdom perspective, we honor our leaders and obey them to the glory of God. Elijah the prophet was an anointed and bold man. Elijah prayed that there would be no rain for three and a half years, and there was no rain. And then he prayed that there should be rain, and there was rain. The guy had a relationship with God so great that when he said, "Oh, God, send fire," *boom!* Fire came!

The only way Elisha, his servant, was going to have the anointing was to serve. There was no other way. When you serve the leaders in the church, and when you serve the man and the woman of God, the anointing rubs off on you. Elisha received the anointing because he served Elijah. Timothy received the anointing because he served Paul.

There is no other way. Let's take away all expectation that one can be a person of authority without being *under* authority. That is not the Kingdom of God. In the Kingdom of God, you have to be under authority to have authority. So don't go off doing your own thing, expecting God to bless the work of your hands when you have no authority in and over your life. Christ was submissive to authority, even to John the Baptist. When Jesus went to be baptized, John asked Jesus to baptize him instead. Jesus refused so that the fullness of scripture will be fulfilled.

Who is your spiritual father? Who is your spiritual mother? Who are you connected to? Who are you serving? Whose Bible are you picking up? Whose lawn are you mowing? Who is it that has impacted your life? Who is it that took you under their wing and built you up? When was the last time you called them? Feeling that the Lord has called you is not reason or excuse to break connection. You've got to serve to receive the anointing. You've got to serve it. You've got to serve. In the house of God, the way to anointing is service.

> I'd rather be a doorkeeper in the house of my God than dwell in the tents of wickedness.
> (Psalm 84:10)

Training is sometimes hard. It is easy for us to say that "I will do anything for God," but the very moment you are asked to mop the floor our attitude changes. If you cannot be faithful in that which is little, you cannot be trusted with much. In the kingdom, you repeat a level until you pass the test for that place in the kingdom.

There's no other way. You cannot bribe God. There's nothing you can do to skip steps as you grow in the anointing needed to fulfill the call. You cannot cheat! You must serve your time. And when it comes to serving your time, no matter how long it takes, you must be found faithfully executing the last instruction you received from God.

Three things you must do. First, pray for your pastors and leaders. Second, serve your pastors and leaders. Third, don't leave your post until you are released by God. Until you are released, you do not leave because on the day and in the season that you are released it shall be of God, and you shall have the anointing of your leader and the anointing that God has on your life. That's where the double portion comes from. The double portion anointing does not come by request, it comes by being *sweetly broken* by several years of service and heart preparation. Because I have to serve, I will serve so that I can fulfill my destiny. Folks, we have agreed; there is no other way.

CHAPTER 7

INTO THE WILDERNESS

*Then Jesus was led by the Spirit into the desert to
be tempted by the devil.*

—*Matthew 4:1*

Every man or woman of God with a true call on their
lives goes through seasons we've come to know as the
wilderness. One warm summer day in 2005, I boarded
the bus from Norfolk, Virginia, to Alexandria, Virginia.
Sitting alone on the front row seat, I read the book *Power
Healing* by John Wimber. In the introduction by Richard
Foster, he wrote, "I have been seeking God to raise up an
incendiary company of Spirit-led, Spirit-ordained, Spirit-
trained, leaders . . . leaders who are, lone like the Tishbite
(Elijah), like the Baptist (John) bold; cast in a rare and
apostolic mold." For some reason, I began to tear up. I
believe it was an acknowledgment that the call of God
will require me to be alone like the Tishbite. It is my firm
conviction that what is termed the wilderness experience
is that time in our walk with God when the road becomes

narrow, wide enough for only you and God. All others fall away, howbeit temporarily, so God can have his fullest and most personal time with you.

MY FIRST WILDERNESS

After leaving the shores of Ghana and being separated from my parents and siblings, I felt a degree of loneliness and separation. It was a trying time adjusting to a new culture, weather, and people. Every fifteen-year-old leaving his parents to go to a foreign land across great bodies of water will feel the same way I did. It was difficult nonetheless, but that season does not compare to a wilderness experience that lasted an entire year, beginning in June 1998. Up until that time, I had never taken a day off from school. I had received my admission letter from the Ohio State University and was extremely excited. When I found out I could not go because of financial reasons, I was very disappointed. It was no fault of mine, but I had to live with that reality. This shocking truth ignited a season of breaking and rebuilding in my life.

First, I had to overcome the victim mentality that everyone was out to get me or at least to slow me down. All my peers would be a year ahead of me, and I felt left behind. Sometimes I would say, "If only my dad was here." Dad was always there to make sure school fees were paid and my education was never interrupted. This time, the road was wide enough for only my Heavenly Father and me. I had to walk through this without human assistance.

The wilderness experience strips you of competition and comparison to others as your indication of your success.

I began to look at myself more as an individual with God, rather than as part of this clan of people. Without people, who are you? You will answer this question in the wilderness.

A few months into the summer, I was working two jobs as a cashier in a grocery store and as a sales associate at an office supplies store. It was a hectic schedule for a seventeen-year-old boy who really wanted to go to college. There were times that I arrived at one store at 6:00 a.m., completed my shift at 3:00 p.m., ran home, ate, showered, then ran to the other job to work from 4:00 p.m. till 9:00 p.m. Instead of studying economics from books, I did so by mopping floors, bagging groceries, and selling office furniture. God stripped away the "why me?" mentality. In this wilderness, God made me realize that I was not abandoned. He was my ever-present help in my time of need. Adversity does not mean abandonment!

It was at these jobs that I learned work discipline, customer service, and business protocol. These same bosses who provoked character growth in me also gave me the greatest compliments. These compliments were to me like drops of water in that dry season of my life. I saw glimmers of hope, and I felt I was somebody. My time would come! (Habakkuk 2:1-3). I declare over you right now that your time will come, in Jesus's name! You are blessed of God and certainly not forgotten!

Paychecks came weekly. I saved some money, bought groceries for the home, bought school supplies (I knew where I was going), and some clothes. The most important financial lesson I learned during this wilderness was paying my first tithe. It was the greatest feeling to actually be able to practice what I believed and preached. I have not stopped tithing since. Giving a tenth of my income plus my offering is an expression of my confidence in God and because God commands it. Truthfully, any hesitation about paying your tithe to your local church is not a money or church problem, it's your heart. Check yourself!

The dictionary description of a *wilderness* is a wild place untouched by human development. There is wildness about the place that causes us to reconsider ways of doing things and focusing on the priorities. In the wilderness, you feel alone, out of place, abandoned, disoriented, and inadequate and not in control. Welcome to the transformation chamber! Here, all wild urges and out-of-control personalities are brought under the authority of Jesus Christ.

ENJOYING ALONENESS

In the last days and hours of Jesus's life on earth, He experienced immense separation from everyone. His brothers and sisters, the Jews, were against Him. The religious authorities were plotting to kill him. His disciples were sleeping when He needed them to pray. The Roman soldiers were about to crucify Him and plunge a spear through His side. His Father was about to separate from Him for a moment while He carried and destroyed the world's sin that He carried. Jesus knew all of this, yet after crying and weeping, He concluded, "Nevertheless not My will but Your will be done." His ministry journey began with forty days in the wilderness and ended with intense wilderness in the garden and on the cross.

The wilderness experience is God's personal time to break off the old and replenish with the new. The only way to endure and reap the full benefits of the wilderness is to embrace it and enjoy the aloneness with God. Consider it your personal encounter with God—a time for equipping you for the task at hand. Jesus's wilderness at thirty prepared Him for the ministry. His wilderness in the garden of Gethsemane prepared Him for the cross. His wilderness on the cross prepared Him for eternal glory.

> And being found in appearance as a man, He humbled himself and became obedient to death—even death on a cross! Therefore God exalted Him to the highest place and gave Him the name that is above every name, that at the name of Jesus every knee should bow, in heaven and on earth and under the earth, and every tongue confess that Jesus Christ is Lord, to the glory of God the Father (Philippians 2:8-11).

Just like Jesus, let's embrace and enjoy the wilderness knowing:

> Our light and momentary troubles are achieving for us an eternal glory that far outweighs them all (2 Corinthians 4:17).

> Let us fix our eyes on Jesus, the Author and Perfecter of our faith, who for the joy set before him endured the cross, scorning its shame, and

sat down at the right hand of the throne of God.
Consider him who endured such opposition
from sinful men, so that you will not grow weary
and lose heart (Hebrews 12:2-3).

The wilderness experience is very much God-initiated.
You will normally be well into a wilderness experience
before you consciously know that you are. It is all part
of God's design. If you knew you were about to enter the
wilderness, you will most likely want to delay it by a few
days, weeks, months, or years . . . truth be told. So how do
you know when you are in the wilderness of God? These
are three signs of a God-initiated wilderness experience.

SIGN 1: The people who used to understand you no longer
do.

PURPOSE: At the end of the wilderness, you will have a
renewed vision and a new group of people (eagles) to help
you accomplish it. "He who walks with the wise grows
wise, but a companion of fools suffers harm" (Proverbs
13:20).

SIGN 2: The activities that used to be fun and pleasurable
fade away

PURPOSE: A change of appetite comes with the wilderness
package. A hunger and thirst for God alone is needed to
deliver God's gift to you. "Blessed are those who hunger and
thirst for righteousness, for they will be filled" (Matthew
5:6).

SIGN 3: Your weaknesses and character flaws become glaringly obvious to you.

PURPOSE: A higher level of character is required for the new level of anointing. God will expose you to yourself so you can humble yourself to Him and be repaired. "Blessed is the man whom God corrects; so do not despise the discipline of the Almighty" (Job 5:17).

The wilderness experience is continual because we are a work in progress. It is not only spiritual; it is physical, emotional, social, and in every area of your life. To walk with God, we will constantly need a person makeover. Expect it, embrace it, and enjoy it.

Let's process the experience of two patriarchs, Joseph and Moses, when they were led into the wilderness to be perfected for their life-long assignments. We'll observe the three signs of a wilderness experience and how they responded to them. You are not alone!

JOSEPH: FROM CANAAN TO EGYPT

Joseph enjoyed the maximum attention he needed and wanted from his father, Jacob. He was his favorite son, and he wore the one and only special, custom-made coat of many colors. He was loved, and he was a dreamer who willingly shared his dreams. Then God's next plan for Joseph was set in motion.

SIGN 1: The people who used to understand you no longer do.

Joseph's brothers no longer saw him as one of them. His dreams had pushed them to the brink of hatred. Jacob, their father, also joins the boys after Joseph's latest dream. The people who once understood Joseph no longer did. To them, his words, actions, and dreams were extreme and weird. That is how it is with your wilderness. Those who thought they had you figured out soon realize they don't. Please note that this will frustrate and irritate them, but you must continue to obey God.

> SIGN 2: The activities that used to be fun and pleasurable fade away.

Joseph had a pretty comfortable lifestyle. The most he did was to send food to his brothers when they worked in the fields. I would imagine that he did not allow his designer coat to be soiled by the daily activities of farm life. When he was thrown into a pit and sold into slavery, he lost his coat and woke up to a whole new world of living. His life got replaced with floor scrubbing, market shopping, toilet cleaning, and sheep shearing. Let's not forget some jail time and a real-time realization of how soon man forgets what is done for them. What used to be fun and pleasure faded away. We would notice the maturity of Joseph in Egypt. The attention on him shifted to focus on God. He declared before Pharaoh, "It is not in me; God will give Pharaoh a favorable answer" (Genesis 41:16). That was only possible because his hunger shifted from life pleasures and himself to knowing God and helping others.

> SIGN 3: Your weaknesses and character flaws become
> glaringly obvious to you.

Joseph's character and resolve to please God was strengthened in his time in Egypt. I am not aware of any specific weaknesses Joseph had, but we know he did because he was human. The strength of character is evidenced by the favor of God and the favor of man upon him. Whatever Joseph did prospered (Genesis 39:5-6). Potiphar, his master, made him plenipotentiary over his entire estate. Later on, Pharaoh did the same. Even when thrown in jail, he found favor before the keeper of the prison. When advising Pharaoh concerning the famine to come, Joseph did not toot his own horn. He told Pharaoh to find a man to execute this survival plan. What great humility! It was a sign of a man whose character had been processed. Another proof Joseph's character was fortified by his wilderness experience was his reaction to his brothers when they came to Egypt for grain. He acknowledged the journey of his personal wilderness was God's plan to save his family.

> Then Joseph said to his brothers, "Come close to me." When they had done so, he said, "I am your brother Joseph, the one you sold into Egypt! And now, do not be distressed and do not be angry with yourselves for selling me here, because it was to save lives that God sent me ahead of you. For two years now there has been famine in the land, and for the next five years there will not be

plowing and reaping. But God sent me ahead of
you to preserve for you a remnant on earth and
to save your lives by a great deliverance. So then,
it was not you who sent me here, but God. He
made me father to Pharaoh, lord of his entire
household and ruler of all Egypt." (Genesis
45:4-8)

MOSES: FROM EGYPT TO MIDIAN

Moses had his socioeconomic status changed within
ninety days of his life. He became a member of the royal
family of the greatest country in the world at that time.
Moses escaped becoming a slave and gained instant access
to the best education possible. In human eyes, Moses had
it going for him. Then God's next plan for Moses was
initiated.

SIGN 1: The people who used to understand you no
longer do.

Moses became restless when he knew he was a Hebrew
and saw his fellow Hebrews being tormented through
slavery. I could picture Moses asking questions of both
Egyptians and Hebrews. He no doubt asked his adoptive
mother numerous questions to understand who he was. He
later killed an Egyptian and had to flee Egypt. The royal
court was stunned. What has come over Moses? Why does
he spend so much time with the slaves? The Hebrews on
the other hand might have also wondered why this Egyptian

was always over at their place and doing favors for them. It's a trap, he's a spy, many may have thought. All of a sudden, those who understood Moses no longer did. Those with whom he had things in common could not see him as one of them. Egypt wanted Moses dead!

SIGN 2: The activities that used to be fun and pleasurable fade away.

Moses's job description changed from general in the Egyptian military to keeper of sheep at the backside of the desert. Moses's appetite began to change in his last days in Egypt. He hungered for justice and freedom. The niceties of his birth country were no longer fulfilling. He hoped there was more to life than that. In his wilderness experience, Moses traded his Egyptian scrolls for classroom sheep. He was the student. The lesson topics included but were not limited to the following: "Quiet, God is Speaking," "How to Navigate Impossible Terrain," "How to Defend and Protect Sheep," and "Loving, Forgiving, and Guiding Rebel Sheep."

SIGN 3: Your weaknesses and character flaws become glaringly obvious to you.

Moses had an anger problem. He killed a man in Egypt, he destroyed the first set of Ten Commandments tablets, and he struck the rock when God asked him to speak to it. In the wilderness, Moses was forced to confront that

troublesome area of his life. Justified anger was no excuse
to destroy things. He learned that quick and fast results did
not apply to people—one of the many lessons he acquired
from hanging out with sheep. In his encounter with God at
the burning bush, Moses realized that strength and might
were not the answer to everything. God exposed Moses's
inadequacies, and then affirmed him that he, Moses, was
able to accomplish the mission because He, the "I AM
THAT I AM" was with him.

At the end of the wilderness experience, you would:

- be humbled,
- have greater confidence and reliance on God,
- lose some friends,
- have greater and refined character.

The wilderness is a place between you and the
manifestation of God's promise in your life. Until you
embrace and enjoy the wilderness, your ability to handle
God's best for you is, at best, weak and incomplete. Let
God have His way with and in you. Accept this invitation
to the wilderness. It is only those who are *sweetly broken*
by God in the wilderness who understand, appreciate, and
truly know His *love*, *power*, and *grace*!

CHAPTER 8

SWEETLY BROKEN

Fresh from the wilderness, you feel like a new person. The old you with its fleshly attitude is broken, and you are ready to embark on a wild adventure of knowing God and doing His will. Welcome to an exhilarating new beginning!

The number 8 in numerology is understood as the number of new beginnings. With 7 being the number of completion and perfection, 8 logically is the renewal of a cycle. Chapter 8 is appropriately titled "Sweetly Broken" because it is very central to your success in life and ministry. It is in many ways a road map and guide about what is yet to come and how you can specifically navigate through it. With an open heart and teachable spirit, let's explore two major seasons you will experience in your journey to fulfill God's assignment for you: seasons of insignificance and seasons of humility.

SEASONS OF INSIGNIFICANCE

It is in the seasons of insignificance that God works out the true intent and purposes of our hearts. Picture this: You make a commitment to serve others. You try to be nice to others; keep quiet when at former times you would have lashed back. You turn the other cheek, but then no one seems to notice. Your ideas, hard work, and dedication to your areas of ministry are evident to you (because you know how you were six months ago), but still no one notices. To add to that, people start giving you flak and talking about you, and you feel like giving them a piece of your mind (but you can't because it is the mind of Christ you have). On top of that, the people you clearly know are not doing as much as you are publicly honored and you feel unappreciated and wonder if you should keep serving. That is just a taste of a season of insignificance. It comes in two ways: wrong motives and God-initiated.

WRONG MOTIVES

When we work for the applause of men, we set ourselves up for disappointment. Our motives cannot be to let everyone see how awesome we are and pat us on the back. Remember, the same folks saying "Hosanna" also cried out "Crucify Him." You probably agree based on a recent experience you've had. The crowd is fickle, and the applause of men is conditional and guaranteed to fade. Jesus admonishes us not to let the left hand know what the right hand is doing. He warns us not to be like the Pharisees who give their alms in public so all might see.

"Unless your righteousness exceeds that of the Pharisees, you would not enter the kingdom of God" (Matthew 5:20). To expect honor and recognition from men is to be a Pharisee. Change your motives toward public admiration and serve God alone.

GOD-INITIATED

God will intentionally withhold recognition from us to see where our heart truly lies. He allowed Job to go through his conditions to confirm that his heart was right. God loves you and does not want you to fall victim to pride, the precursor to a fall. Until you are numb to the praises of men, you are susceptible to pride. By allowing you to serve and obey without public reward, you truly live your life for an audience of one. Whether man sees, does not see, or chooses not to see is irrelevant to you because you know whose you are and whom you serve. God purifies us through the season of insignificance to keep our motives right and to stir us away from pride.

SEASONS OF HUMILITY

If there is one word I have heard ministered, taught, counseled, and preached to me personally over and over again, it is humility. My father, my mentors, my congregation, and God continually admonish me to be humble. It is important if you are going to last and actually finish your divine assignment. When I speak with my father on the telephone, he'll end our conversation by reminding me to humble myself and honor those around me. He said it so much it finally sunk in, and I totally took hold of it.

I was admonished by the Lord that none of His plans for my life will be fulfilled outside of humility. I have had others confirm this to me as well. Now, I do not consider these admonishments as a rebuke. On the contrary, I receive them as God's preventive medicine for pride.

Jesus is the perfect example of humility. If He did it and was commended for it, we must do the same.

> Your attitude should be the same as that of Christ Jesus: Who, being in very nature God, did not consider equality with God something to be grasped, but made Himself nothing, taking the very nature of a servant, being made in human likeness. And being found in appearance as a man, He humbled Himself and became obedient to death—even death on a cross! Therefore God exalted Him to the highest place and gave Him the name that is above every name, that at the name of Jesus every knee should bow, in heaven and on earth and under the earth, and every tongue confess that Jesus Christ is Lord, to the glory of God the Father." (Philippians 2:5-11)

Throughout His life, Jesus proved humility. At His baptism, Jesus humbled Himself for John the Baptist, His cousin, to baptize Him in order to fulfill scripture. Listen carefully, my friend. It was to fulfill scripture that Jesus allowed John to baptize Him. John declared that he was unworthy to untie Jesus's shoelaces, but Jesus humbled

Himself anyway. Humility requires you to act and live completely guided by the Word of God. Your opinions and ideas may be great, but they are secondary to the Word of God. That is humility, my friend; when God's Word is the final authority in your life and you obey no matter what or how you feel.

> Humble yourselves before the Lord, and he will
> lift you up. (James 4:10)

Again, Jesus exemplified humility when He took a bowl of water, a towel, and bent His knees to wash His disciples' feet. The sandals they wore in the first century were nothing compared to the shoes, sneakers, alligator, and ostrich boots we have today. Their feet picked up dirt and "other stuff" from everywhere they went. To wash another person's feet was a great undertaking. Yet Jesus, the Rabbi, Teacher, Lord, Savior, and God did not think twice about doing it. The reason is found when Peter indicated his displeasure with Jesus's plan to wash his feet. Stinky feet and stinky pride! Jesus responded, "Unless I wash you, you have no part with me" (John 13:8). Peter quickly relinquished his position. It was because Jesus wanted the bond of unity. He willingly washed feet and served His disciples in order to make us all one with Him. That's humility! What are you doing in your home, marriage, church, school, work place, and community to foster the bond of unity with those God has called you to? He's called you to serve! Will you commit today to serve whomever God sends you to serve?

Jesus displayed humility again when He cried out "I thirst!" as He was dying on the cross. Many people believe their worth is in their ability to take care of themselves and not depend on others at all. No one is an island, and you will not be effective in the Kingdom of God being isolated from others. By asking for water, Jesus showed us that it is okay to ask for help when we need it. Of course Jesus could have sent legions of angels, made it rain, or satisfied his thirst any way he wanted; but He did not. He asked for help. In true humility, we have to understand our role and the role of others in helping us fulfill God's plan in our lives. Don't try to be a superhero. Ask for help when you need it.

Humility toward God is a place of authority because we acknowledge our inability and then take on His ability. I don't know about you, but I will gladly trade my best for whatever might be God's weakest. His least supersedes my best as far as the east is from the west. It is not the kind of humility that says "Woe is me," but rather humility that takes root in the place of authority and power because you trade your strength for the strength of God. You say, "O God, I humble myself before You so that Your strength will be manifest in my life."

Humility in the body of Christ is a major key to fulfilling your calling because Christ humbled himself, even to the point of death, and His name is exalted high above every name. If we want to walk in that power and in that authority, we must learn how to humble ourselves.

> Therefore if there is any encouragement in
> Christ, if there is any consolation of love, if there

is any fellowship of the spirit, if any affection and
compassion, make my joy complete by being the
same mind, maintaining the same love, united in
spirit, intent on one purpose. Do nothing from
selfishness or empty conceit, but with humility
of mind regard one another as more important
than yourself. Do not look merely out for your
own personal interest, but also for the interest
of others. (Philippians 2:1-4)

When God showed me that understanding of what the
body of Christ was, I got excited for the person next to me
because I now understood that if Bobby makes it, I make
it. That if Susan does well, I do well. So I'll be praying for
you and I'll be pushing you forward because together we
succeed. Let's put aside that competitive, "I am better than
you" and "I have to get more than you" mentality.

For through the grace given to me, I say to
everyone among you not to think more highly
of himself than he ought to think. But to think
so as to have some judgment as God has allotted
to each a measure of faith. For just as we have
many members in one body and all the members
do not have the same function so we who are
many are one body in Christ and individually
one of another. (Romans 12:3-5)

Your life, your relationship with the person next to you
is very important because we all have different gifts.

"For I was hungry and you gave me something to eat, I was thirsty and you gave me something to drink, I was a s stranger and you invited me in, I needed clothes and you clothed me, I was sick and you looked after me, I was in prison and you came to visit me. Then the righteous will answer Him, "Lord, when did we see you hungry and feed you, or thirsty and give you something to drink? When did we see you a stranger and invite you in, or needed clothes and clothe you? When did we see you sick or in prison and go to visit you? The King will reply, "I tell you the truth, whatever you did for one of the least of these brothers of mine, you did to me." (Matthew 25: 35-40)

God is saying whatever you've done to each member you have done to me. In Zechariah the Bible says you are the apple of God's eye. I am the apple of Gods eye. Your brother is the apple of God's eye. Your sister is the apple of God's eye. So whatever you do to the next person you do unto God. You must put your desire for all the big things aside if you cannot treat your neighbor right especially in the body of Christ.

The seasons of humility are constant and continual. It is a choice and intent of the will to be humble. It's not automatic to the flesh. Discipline yourself to consider (value, embrace, regard, respect and honor) others more than yourself, and let the love of Christ shine through you as you serve.

FINAL EXHORTATION

I have a lot more to share with you, but the Holy Spirit has instructed me to end the book here. When He gives me the freedom, it would be my privilege to share more with you. The time of the Lord's coming is near. Surrender yourself to the processing of God. Be *sweetly broken* so you can be fit for the Master's use. May it never be said of you that you had potential but never fulfilled God's plan for your life. By going through the pathway we've discussed in this book, your potential will be released, and the hand of God will direct you to fulfill His plan for your life.

MOSES AND JOSHUA

No one will be able to stand up against you all the days of your life. As I was with Moses, so I will be with you; I will never leave you nor forsake you. Have I not commanded you? Be strong and courageous. Do not be terrified; do not be discouraged, for the Lord your God will be with you wherever you go.

—Joshua 1:5, 9

Joshua was chosen and trained by Moses with the intention that he will take over from him. When Moses chose Joshua, he kept him close to himself. Joshua also had a personal drive to know God. It is a similar passion for God while we serve that will prepare and sustain you for the entire calling.

Then Moses summoned Joshua and said to
him in the presence of all Israel, "Be strong
and courageous, for you must go with this
people into the land that the Lord swore to
their forefathers to give them, and you must
divide it among them as their inheritance."
(Deuteronomy 31:7)

JOSHUA STAYED IN GOD'S PRESENCE

After Moses and Joshua had finished communing with
God in the Tent of Meeting, Moses left. Joshua, however,
stayed in God's presence. Without your mentors or in their
absence, you must willingly and continually stay in the
presence of God. The presence of God is what distinguishes
you (Exodus 33:11-16).

JOSHUA WAS READY

Moses died before he could set foot in the Promised
Land. Moses lived for one hundred and twenty years, but
his eyes were not weak or his strength gone. Be ready to
take God's people to the next level when your mentor,
father, or mother is called on to a different assignment.
Do not waste time idling around now because the time of
the call is God's decision. Learn all you can and be ready
in season and out of season. At all times with or without

your mentor, in leadership or in training, be a leader; remain humble!

> "It is not by might nor by power but by My Spirit says the Lord" (Zechariah 4:6).

Mighty blessings!

STUDY

GUIDE

FOR

SWEETLY

BROKEN

FOREWORD

1. What three application lessons did you learn?
2. If you wrote the foreword to this book, what would it say?

CHAPTER 1: BORN FOR SUCH A TIME AS THIS

1. What is your life mission statement?
2. Write down the story behind your name.
3. What is your birth date? What day of the week was it?
4. Describe the circumstance surrounding your birth.
5. Name the four truths about God-initiated visions. Explain them in your own words.
6. Why do godly visions NOT bake any faster despite the urgency to share the gospel in our time?
7. Write down 7 new biblical declarations concerning your life. Read it out loud daily.

CHAPTER 2: SMALL BEGINNINGS

1. Write out 5 stories which remind you of or indicate your small beginnings.
2. How do failure and setbacks contribute to your preparation for the call?
3. What does this mean to you: "Do not despise small beginnings"?

4. How is your current situation a "small beginning"?

CHAPTER 3: THE ANATOMY OF THE CALL

1. What are the two types of calling? Which one applies to you and how?
2. What are the common themes in a call?
3. List the six C's of the call. Explain each.
4. What is your response to the discussion on *potential?*
5. List all the areas in your life that are *potential.* What do you intend to do about them?
6. Who has confirmed the call of God upon your life? What did they say?
7. Describe as specific as possible, what the fruit of your potential looks like. How would your life story be told?

CHAPTER 4: NOTICING THE CALL

1. Why is timing important in the fulfillment of the call?
2. Write the general guidelines for prophetic words.
3. Describe three or more life experiences you've had that provide hints for your call.
4. What do these hints of your call reveal?
5. Create a timeline of your life. You will be amazed at what you discover!

6. What adversities have you overcome that unmistakably link to the call?
7. Describe briefly the role of adversity in identifying the call of God.

CHAPTER 5: PROCESSING THE CALL

1. How are you intentionally processing God's call on your life?
2. Are you wrestling with God? Who's winning?
3. What was God's response to Jeremiah's whining?
4. Do you have enough resources now to fulfill your divine assignment? If yes, is the assignment God-sized? If no, how do you feel right now?
5. Apart from concerns about self-confidence and finances, what other hesitations do you have as you process the assignment?
6. Discuss *peace*.
7. How close are you to?

CHAPTER 6: YES LORD! NOW WHAT?

1. What are the advantages of formal training? Any disadvantages?
2. Are there alternatives to formal education in the call God has for you?
3. What is God saying about your life preparation for the assignment?

4. Do you have anyone who has and can challenge your perspective on the call? If not, who could you ask to be your accountability partner or mentor?
5. Discuss: "Skip training and service and you become a liability and casualty of ministry."
6. Define humility?
7. How do you relate to your current leaders?
8. "You cannot be in authority unless you are under authority." What does this mean to you?
9. How does instruct as to respond to unjust leadership?

CHAPTER 7: INTO THE WILDERNESS

1. If you told the story of your first experience, what would we hear?
2. What did you learn while you were in the?
3. How does differ from?
4. In the the path of the call becomes wide enough for only you and God. Discuss this statement.
5. What counsel would you give to someone experiencing the?

CHAPTER 8: SWEETLY BROKEN

1. What two ways do we experience seasons of insignificance? How does this resonate with your life?
2. Study and note seven ways by which Jesus exemplified humility?

3. What is false humility? Are you guilty of it?
4. Are you ready to be? What must you do next?
5. Ministry flows out of our lives, not our lives out of ministry. Do you agree or disagree?
6. Who are your mentors?
7. Who are you mentoring?
8. Are you ready and equipped to be a mentor?

IN YOUR HONEST OPINION

Feedback is the breakfast of champions! So I want to hear from you. I will be grateful when you take the time to email your responses to the following questions to me.
Email: *pastormoses@lolcc.org* Thank you!

1. What was your overall experience reading?
2. How could I further impart the revelation in this book?
3. How relevant is this message to our time?
4. Would you like to see this book taught at seminars, conferences, and church or ministry event?

Once again, thank you very much! I pray you were mightily impacted by this book as your walk the journey of being to fulfill the call of God on your life. I invite you to join the discussion on Facebook [Sweetly Broken – The Book]. Mighty Blessings!